ESTRENO CONTEMPORARY SPANISH PLAYS

General Editor

Phyllis Zatlin
Professor of Spanish
Rutgers, The State University of New Jersey

Advisory Board

Sharon Carnicke
Professor of Theatre and
Associate Dean
University of Southern California

Martha Halsey
Professor of Spanish
The Pennsylvania State University

Sandra Harper
Editor, *Estreno*
Ohio Wesleyan University

Marion Peter Holt
Critic and Translator
New York City

Steven Hunt
Associate Professor of Theatre
Converse College

Felicia Hardison Londré
Curators' Professor of Theatre
University of Missouri – Kansas City
American Theatre Fellow

Christopher Mack
Writer and Director
Paris

Grant McKernie
Professor of Theatre
University of Oregon

ESTRENO Collection of Contemporary Spanish Plays

General Editor: Phyllis Zatlin

IGNACIO DEL MORAL

DARK MAN'S GAZE

(La mirada del hombre oscuro)

A MOMMY AND A DADDY

(Papis)

LITTLE BEARS

(Oseznos)

Translated from the Spanish
by
Jartu Gallashaw Toles

ESTRENO Plays
New Brunswick, New Jersey
2005

ESTRENO Contemporary Spanish Plays 27
General Editor: Phyllis Zatlin
                  Department of Spanish & Portuguese
                  Faculty of Arts & Sciences
                  Rutgers, The State University of New Jersey
                  105 George Street
                  New Brunswick, New Jersey 08901-1414 USA

Library of Congress Cataloging in Publication Data
Del Moral, Ignacio, 1957-
   Dark Man's Gaze and Other Plays
   Bibliography:
   Contents: Dark Man's Gaze. A Mommy and a Daddy. Little Bears.
Translations of: La mirada del hombre oscuro. Papis. Oseznos.
   1. Del Moral, Ignacio, 1957-
         Translation, English.
I. Toles, Jartu Gallashaw. II. Title.
Library of Congress Control No.: 2004114689
ISBN: 1-888463-19-8

Published with support from
Program for Cultural Cooperation
Between Spain's Ministry of Education, Culture and Sports and
United States Universities

Cover: Jeffrey Eads

TABLE OF CONTENTS

ABOUT THE PLAYWRIGHT

Ignacio del Moral was born in 1957 in San Sebastián. His involvement in the theatre began in 1974 as a member of the Aula de Teatro of Madrid's Universidad Autónoma. Following a brief period in the late 1970s as an actor with the company of Manuel Canseco and the Teatro Libre, under the direction of José Luis Alonso de Santos, Del Moral turned to writing for the stage and television. His first play, *La gran muralla* (The Great Wall), is a work for children. Written in 1982, it debuted in 1988. To date he has authored nearly two dozen plays, of which half have been published and nearly all have been performed.

La gran muralla provides the first glimpse of the interplay of the three elements that come to define Del Moral's theatre as a whole: fantasy or illusion, humor, and didacticism. Whether his other plays for children such as *Sabina y las brujas* (Sabina and the Witches), his more satirical works such as *Soledad y ensueño de Robinsón Crusoe* (Robinson Crusoe's Solitude and Dreams), or works in which he experiments with dramatic form and narrative structure such as *Fugadas* (Flights) and *Páginas arrancadas del diario de P* (Pages from P's Diary), Del Moral is motivated by a deep sense of social and artistic consciousness. Driven by a desire to educate, the author leads his audiences to an exploration of what lies beneath the surface, thereby inviting a confrontation with certain facets of the human condition that may otherwise go unnoticed.

Del Moral's theatre is characterized by a calculated integration of text, context, and form and the opposition of stylistic and thematic nuances. In *A Mommy and a Daddy*, for example, the encounter between the two characters of the play eludes discursive thought; it leads us to believe that reality is relative at best and, as a result, that human interaction is little more than incidental. Reality and fantasy are counterpoised but at the same time fused in a manner to suggest that life and art emerge from a sense of discovery both on the part of the characters and the spectators. *Little Bears* is founded on two oppositional paradigms: humor vs. bleak reality and self vs. other. The play deals with the impact of violence on the individual, society, and human interaction. Albeit a disturbing picture of human nature, what transpires in the play ultimately suggests that there is hope that personal and social transgressions can be overcome if we are willing to be educated. The real and

IGNACIO DEL MORAL
Photo by Phyllis Zatlin

the fictitious are again skillfully fused in *Dark Man's Gaze* and *Rey Negro* (The Black King), plays in which Del Moral posits a universal message about human behavior. Dramatic tension in the play derives from the opposition of social commitment and social disengagement. The behavior of the characters in both plays, like many individuals in society, comes across as scripted. Irony is a major feature of both works, employed by Del Moral to reveal that difference breeds hypocrisy.

Ignacio del Moral's works represent one of the more socially conscious dramatic expressions of present day Spain. Convinced that it is never too late to instruct, Del Moral is committed to holding a mirror up to society in an effort to unmask our petty insecurities, quell our fears, and disprove beliefs that very often have no base in reality. Challenging long held convictions and traditional practices is no easy task. Del Moral understands, however, that certain facets of society must first be made visible in order to move us toward a deeper understanding of human nature, cultural beliefs and practices, and social and political ideologies.

John P. Gabriele
The College of Wooster

La mirada del hombre oscuro (*Dark Man's Gaze*), Sala Olimpia, Madrid, 1993. Dir. by Ernesto Caballero. Photo by Manuel Martínez Muñoz.

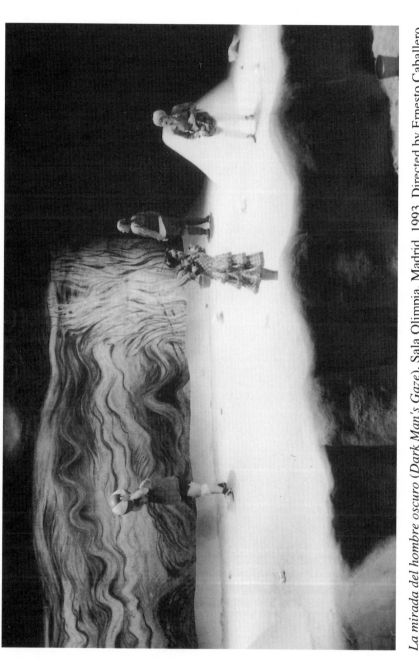

La mirada del hombre oscuro (*Dark Man's Gaze*). Sala Olimpia, Madrid, 1993. Directed by Ernesto Caballero. Set design by Amador Méndez. Photo by Manuel Martínez Muñoz.

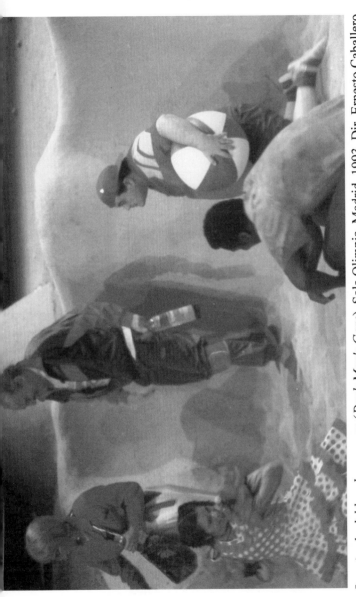

La mirada del hombre oscuro (*Dark Man's Gaze*). Sala Olimpia, Madrid, 1993. Dir. Ernesto Caballero. Set design Amador Méndez. Photo by Chicho, courtesy of Centro de Documentación Teatral.

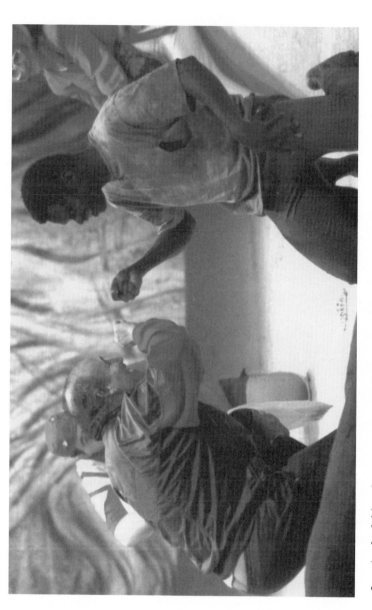

La mirada del hombre oscuro (Dark Man's Gaze). Dir. Ernesto Caballero. Photo by Chicho, courtesy of Centro de Documentación Teatral.

A NOTE ON THE PLAYS

Ignacio del Moral courageously tackles the subject of man's gregarious nature: that fundamental need for human connection. While many playwrights are accused of reviewing the same thematic chord throughout their careers, few are as adept as he at examining their subjects across such an expansive divide. Del Moral challenges his audience to consider how the variables of gender, race, language, age, marital status, and societal norms exacerbate an individual's sense of isolation.

Dark Man's Gaze presents a bleak view of connections thwarted by poor communication. The characters are challenged to overcome the obstacles of foreign language and bias. With the exception of Ombasi, all are without formal names. Ombasi has chosen to leave his native land in search of opportunity. The search lands him marooned on the shores of Spain. He is an outsider, a stranger in a strange land. He is resourceful, generous, and intelligent. However, his misfortune is to be both Black and without command of their language while needing to connect with the generic White Europeans. His attempts to interact with the natives of this new country are met with suspicion, verbal abuse and ultimately violence.

Here, race and gender act as kindling for a volatile explosion. Each of the nameless characters represents a separate faction of the country's body politic, with Father representing the far right and Little Girl being the undecided. None of them is equipped to assist Ombasi as he attempts to construct a bridge across the racial and political divide. The father in fact wages a turf war that escalates into chaos for everyone. Only in the ending does the playwright suggest any hope for resolve to this connection dilemma: life in the metaphysical realm.

In *A Mommy and a Daddy,* Del Moral once again offers generic characters, "Mom" and "Dad." Their lack of formal names suggests a sense of universality. They could be any and every new parent dissatisfied with their spouse. Reminiscent of the Everyman character from Morality plays, Mom and Dad are easily recognizable because of their familiar plight. Their specific yearning is for more emotional support. Fundamentally, they both need complete fulfillment in a relationship. Their cryptic exchange suggests that they might be able to find that in each other. Unfortunately they are married to others and have children with others. Their potential for connection is doomed.

Papis (A Mommy and a Daddy), Sala Olimpia, Madrid, 1992. Directed by Jesús Cracio. Photo by Manuel Martínez Muñoz.

Del Moral paints an intimate view of how difficult breaking through the artifice of socially acceptable exchange can be for men and women (especially those with familial obligations). Mom and Dad share a superficial dialogue that has a terribly poignant subtext. Beneath their polite conversation, "the alibi" of children's health, parental obligations, seagulls and an unfinished thesis, the two flirt with each other. They flirt with their ideal spouse. However, because they are both governed by their "married to another" status, their conversation remains shallow. The ideal, sensitive communicative spouse remains a fantasy, forever existing as an idea. Regardless of their restrictions, there is still the constant attempt to connect. That connection offers a promise of greener grass.

With each story, Del Moral reviews this longing for connection with a different demographic. Only with *Little Bears* do we get a glimpse of hopeful resolve. Here the variables hindering the quest for human connection provide the most destructive as well as the most encouraging results.

Three adolescent males, from dysfunctional families, are under the influence of alcohol; with raging hormones and burgeoning sexualities, they struggle with expressing their intimacy towards each other. These circumstances serve as both the impetus for connection as well as obstacles. The three young men battle each other and their own constitutions with the odds stacked against them. Ultimately, love is the victor, but not without significant loss.

Del Moral's characters are very honest portraits, his language is always immediate, and the tension in each story is palpable. Jartu Toles's translation of these plays allows the reader to experience Del Moral's work as he intended. She has interpreted his plays with an eye towards ascension into theatrical production. The language is clear, compelling, and graphic. Toles has distilled the English language into an amalgamation of pure action. Her exacting choice of words provides the perfect blend for dramatic literature to transcend the shelves of academia.

Here is a perfect marriage: a playwright with a need to exorcise one specific demon and a translator with a gift for incisive language. His continued sermon on this fundamental human need and her selection of words cut to the essence of truth.

Eric Ruffin
Coordinator of the Pre-Directing Program
Theatre Arts Department
Howard University

Inquiries regarding permissions should be addressed to the author through

D. Alfredo Carrión Saiz
Director de Artes Escénicas y Musicales
Sociedad General de Autores y Editores
Fernando VI, 4
28004 Madrid, SPAIN
Phone: 011-34-91-349-96-86   Fax: 011-34-91-349-97-12
E-mail: acarrion@sgae.es

or through the translator:

Jartu Gallashaw Toles
742 Monroe Drive NE #4
Atlanta, GA 30308
E-mail: jtoles1@bellsouth.net

La mirada del hombre oscuro (*Dark Man's Gaze*), recipient of the first annual theatre prize of the Sociedad General de Autores de España in 1991, was first staged in Madrid on 1 August 1993 at the Sala Olimpia. The production was directed by Ernesto Caballero with set design by Amador Méndez. The play was adapted as a movie titled *Bwana* by director Imanol Uribe; winner of the Concha de Oro prize at the San Sebastian Film Festival in 1996, *Bwana* was also chosen as Spain's entry for a foreign film Oscar.

Papis (*A Mommy and a Daddy*) and *Oseznos* (*Little Bears*) were first staged on 3 July 1992 at Madrid's Sala Olimpia as part of an anthology of short plays, *Precipitados*. The production, which also included works by Leopoldo Alas and Ernesto Caballero, was directed by Jesús Cracio. *Oseznos* served as partial inspiration for the film *Barrio* (1998), directed by Fernando León.

Oseznos also was expanded by Del Moral as a full-length play, *La noche del oso* (The Night of the Bear), which premiered in 2003 at the Teatro Arlequín in Madrid, under the direction of Ernesto Caballero.

Ignacio del Moral's

DARK MAN'S GAZE
(LA MIRADA DEL HOMBRE OSCURO)

Translated from the Spanish

by

Jartu Gallashaw Toles

CHARACTERS

THE FAMILY:
    FATHER
    MOTHER
    BOY
    LITTLE GIRL

OMBASI
THE BODY

1. AT THE BEACH

Dusk. Sound of the ocean. A family, with a bucket, is collecting small shellfish. The family includes FATHER, MOTHER, BOY and LITTLE GIRL who plays and lags behind. They work efficiently, lightly raking the sand and uncovering clams to place into the bucket. The family works seriously and mechanically, except the LITTLE GIRL. They are all clad in sweaters and short boots.

The LITTLE GIRL wanders away. SHE climbs up a rather distant dune crowned by thickets and disappears over the other side. They call her and SHE then reappears, running and nervous.

LITTLE GIRL: Dead black men! Dead black men!

MOTHER: Come here, honey, you're going to get lost!

LITTLE GIRL: Dead black men!

BOY: She's stupid!

LITTLE GIRL: Dead black men, Daddy!

FATHER: Just what we needed. She's gone crazy. Yes, sweetie. Go on, see if you find lots of little shells like these. *(To MOTHER.)* See what a good idea it was to come here? The beach is full of them. No one comes out here.

MOTHER: Aren't we too far from the car? I wonder if . . .

FATHER: It'll be fine. No one's here.

MOTHER: It'll be fine? Look what happened to my sister. Now she doesn't have a car. When they went to go get it, it had been stolen.

FATHER: Who's going to come way out here to steal our car? Besides, I take out the spark plug when I leave it. See? *(Showing it to her.)* It won't start without it.

LITTLE GIRL *(Looking for shells but keeping her eyes on the dunes)*: Is this a good one?

FATHER: No, it has to be whole, with both halves. See? The clam has to be in its little house.

(The LITTLE GIRL, paying no attention, throws the empty shell in the bucket.)

MOTHER: What are you doing? Didn't your father tell you that those weren't any good?

LITTLE GIRL: Why?

MOTHER: Because you can't eat them! Because there's no clam!

LITTLE GIRL: How come there's no clam?

BOY: Because it's dead!

LITTLE GIRL: Like the dead black men?

MOTHER: This child will be the death of me!
LITTLE GIRL: Like the black men!
BOY: You are stupid. Stupid! Stupid! Stupid!

> *(The BOY throws fistfuls of wet sand at the LITTLE GIRL. SHE cries. MOTHER shakes the BOY and FATHER mutters.)*

MOTHER: These darn kids! Behave yourselves or you're going to get it!
LITTLE GIRL: Did the black men's mommy kill them?
FATHER: What's with this child and black men?
LITTLE GIRL: Dead black men! Dead black men!

2. BEHIND THE DUNE

Stretched out behind the dune lie two black men. One of them, his eyes half open, does not respond to the fly beginning to lay eggs in a wound on his lip. He must be dead. The other, OMBASI, stirs. He sits up, spits, and vomits salt water. Then he turns toward his companion. Looking at him, OMBASI shoos away the fly. He desperately shakes his companion's body, then sobs silently.OMBASI hears the muddled voices of the shellfishing family. He becomes anxious upon hearing the LITTLE GIRL shout, "dead black men," and the BOY say, "stupid, stupid, stupid."

OMBASI, unsure, glances at his dead companion. Doubtful at first, he removes the other's shoes and places them on his own bare feet. The FAMILY's voices move closer. Finally, the BOY climbs the dune and peers over. HE stares at OMBASI who is trying to remove the dead man's jacket—in better condition than the ragged T-shirt covering his own black chest. The white BOY and the black MAN stare at each other. Terror manifests in the BOY's eyes. The black MAN smiles, ceasing his task. Then, the BOY, momentarily unsure, descends the dune's slope, screaming.

OMBASI climbs his side of the dune in pursuit of the BOY. Screams of the terrified LITTLE GIRL are heard.

3. THE BEACH AND BEYOND

MOTHER and FATHER cease their task at the sound of the BOY's screams. HE runs over, his face full of fright.

FATHER: What's wrong?

MOTHER: Where's your sister?

BOY: There were some black men! There was one black man that had killed the other one!

MOTHER: Where is your sister?

FATHER: What did you say?

MOTHER: Your sister! Where is your sister?

> *(Suddenly OMBASI appears carrying the LITTLE GIRL in his arms. SHE cries. MOTHER screams, FATHER trembles in rage and cowardliness, and OMBASI smiles. HE places the LITTLE GIRL on the ground and SHE runs to the security of her MOTHER. SHE has a wound on her knee, which MOTHER discovers.)*

BOY: Him! He's the one that killed the other one!

MOTHER: What has he done to you?

LITTLE GIRL: He's the dead one! He's the dead one!

FATHER *(Waving a small shovel. OMBASI remains still, cautious)*: Don't move! Get out of here!

OMBASI: The little girl fell . . . She hurt herself.

FATHER *(To the BOY who is still shouting)*: Be quiet, so he doesn't see that we're scared! It'll make things worse. Get away! Leave!

OMBASI *(Pointing to his chest)*: Ombasi. My name is Ombasi.

MOTHER: Let's go.

LITTLE GIRL: What did he say?

MOTHER: Be quiet.

OMBASI: Ombasi. I'm hungry.

FATHER: Go slow. So he can't tell you're afraid.

MOTHER: Where are we going?

FATHER: To the car.

OMBASI: The little girl fell, but it's not serious. I'm hungry. My name is Ombasi. *(To make himself understood, HE points to the LITTLE GIRL, then to himself, then makes an eating gesture.)*

BOY: He's saying he wants to eat her!

(Utterly terrified, the LITTLE GIRL screams and runs. MOTHER runs after her. FATHER confronts OMBASI. The BOY positions himself at a safe distance.)

FATHER: Get out of here! You're scaring my family! Leave! Right now or I'm calling the police!

OMBASI *(Pointing to his chest again)*: Ombasi. I swam here. I'm hungry. My friend drowned. He's dead.

(FATHER listens to him, a bit less tense in light of OMBASI'S seemingly passive attitude.)

FATHER: What did you say?

OMBASI *(After labored concentration, in a terrible accent)*: *Viva España! Sánchez-Vicario!*

FATHER: Well, I'll be damned. Would you listen to this!

MOTHER *(In the distance, holding the LITTLE GIRL'S hand)*: Antonio! Antonio! Leave him alone and let's go before he does something to us! Give him whatever you have and let's go! It's getting dark!

FATHER: Wait! Look what he knows how to say! Say it again.

OMBASI *(Points to his chest again)*: Ombasi.

MOTHER: Are you nuts? Let's go!

FATHER: No! Not that! Viva España!

OMBASI *(Smiling)*: *Viva España! Sánchez-Vicario!*

(The BOY erupts in wild laughter.)

MOTHER: Are you crazy! Let's go! Let's get out of here, it's getting dark and we haven't caught anything!

FATHER: Well, Sánchez-Vicario. I'm leaving. Easy, okay? Everything's fine. We're going. *(Motioning to leave.)*

OMBASI: Wait! *(Going after FATHER.)*

BOY *(Screaming)*: Daddy! He's coming! *(HE runs toward his MOTHER.)*

FATHER *(Turns around, waving the shovel)*: Stop!

OMBASI *(Conciliatory)*: *Viva España . . . Sánchez-Vicario.*

FATHER: Sánchez-Vicario, alright. But you stay here.

OMBASI: My name is Ombasi. I'm hungry. *(He touches his stomach.)*

FATHER *(Calls out to MOTHER)*: Dori! Is there any lunch left?

MOTHER: What for?

FATHER: To give to him.

MOTHER: Why are you going to give our lunch to him?

FATHER: So he'll leave us alone. Maybe he's just hungry.
MOTHER: What if he doesn't like bologna?
FATHER: Then, too bad. Bring it here.

(MOTHER, cautiously, hands FATHER a sandwich wrapped in aluminum foil. FATHER unwraps it and shows it to OMBASI.)

BOY: Why are you giving him my sandwich?
MOTHER: Be quiet!
BOY: No, don't! Daddy is giving my sandwich to that black man who killed the other one.

(OMBASI hesitates and then takes the sandwich that FATHER hands him. HE smiles and eats.)

FATHER: See how he likes bologna?
LITTLE GIRL: I'm hungry! I want a bologna sandwich!
MOTHER: There's a nutella one.
LITTLE GIRL: I don't want nutella! I want bologna!
MOTHER *(To FATHER)*: Why don't you ask him if he minds switching? That way he gets to taste two traditional foods from here.
FATHER: You're crazy! What we have to do is get out of here while we've got him busy. Come on, let's go. It's almost dark.

(The FAMILY members come together, and turning their backs to OMBASI, begin to leave.)

LITTLE GIRL: I'm hungry.
FATHER: Go slow, don't run. Easy.
OMBASI: Don't leave! Wait!
MOTHER: He's going to kill us!
BOY: Just like he killed the other black man.
FATHER *(Turning around)*: Alright, Sánchez-Vicario. What do you want? I've already given you something to eat, right? So, goodbye.
OMBASI: My friend drowned. I don't know where I am.

(OMBASI approaches FATHER, who, scared, empties everything he can find out of his pockets.)

FATHER: Here. I'll give you everything and that's it. See? Take it all and go.
MOTHER: What are you doing?

FATHER: In case he wants to steal. It's better not to stand up to him. Take this, too. *(HE throws everything on the sand. OMBASI looks at him questioningly.)*

MOTHER: Be careful not to toss him the car keys.

FATHER: They're in your purse. *(Suddenly.)* The spark plug.
(HE kneels down and begins to look for it.)

MOTHER: What did you say?

FATHER: I gave him the spark plug.

OMBASI: What's wrong? Are you looking for something?

LITTLE GIRL: I'm going to play, too! *(Beginning to dig in the sand.)*

FATHER: Be still! *(HE shoves the LITTLE GIRL, who cries and seeks refuge in her MOTHER.)*

MOTHER: Don't be so rough!

(OMBASI kneels down beside FATHER.)

BOY: Daddy! Watch out!

(FATHER is frightened for a moment. HE calms down when OMBASI begins to gather everything he'd thrown down and gives it to him.)

OMBASI: Here. And don't throw it down again. Don't be childish.

FATHER: Thanks. The spark plug isn't here . . .

MOTHER: Don't tell me you've lost the spark plug!

FATHER: Well, it isn't here.

MOTHER: What do you mean it isn't there?

FATHER: I mean it isn't here! I don't see it.

MOTHER: But without the spark plug the car won't start, right?

FATHER: Right! *(Once again, HE throws the items on the ground.)* Shit!

OMBASI: Are you going to take me someplace where I can sleep? My friend is dead and I don't know what to do.

MOTHER: Maybe he has it.

FATHER *(To OMBASI)*: Spark plug! For car! *(Makes a gesture as if he's starting the car. OMBASI watches him.)*

MOTHER: Do you really think he's going to understand you?

FATHER *(Continuing to gesture to OMBASI)*: Spark plug for car! Without spark plug the car won't start! Vrrrmm! Vrrrmm!

OMBASI *(Smiling)*: Where do you have it? Let's go before it gets dark! Vrrrmm! Vrrrmm!

MOTHER: See? He's never seen a car in his life!

BOY: Is he from the jungle?

MOTHER: Or from somewhere around there.

FATHER: Goddamn it! (*HE kneels down on the sand and continues to search. It's getting dark.*)

MOTHER: It's getting dark.

LITTLE GIRL: I'm sleepy.

MOTHER: Wait a minute, sweetie, we're about to go right now.

LITTLE GIRL: Why aren't we leaving?

MOTHER: We're leaving soon.

LITTLE GIRL: I want to go now! I want to watch cartoons!

FATHER: Hush her up, she's making me nervous!

MOTHER: Be quiet, sweetie.

BOY: Well, we're going to have to walk back.

FATHER: You, asshole, don't just stand there. Help me look.

OMBASI: Are we going to the car? (*HE kneels beside the man.*) Vrrrmm! Vrrrmmm!

MOTHER: Be careful he doesn't do anything to you.

(*OMBASI begins to collect the same objects that FATHER has thrown down twice and gives them to him.*)

FATHER: I don't want this shit now! I want the spark plug!

(*HE throws the objects again. OMBASI shrugs his shoulders and examines a cigarette lighter, igniting and extinguishing the flame several times.*)

OMBASI: You don't want your lighter?

FATHER: Leave me alone! I'm looking for the spark plug!

OMBASI: Take it. You might need it.

FATHER (*Refusing the lighter*): No! I don't want the lighter! I want the spark plug! Spark plug! (*HE extends his hand.*) Alright! Where is the spark plug? (*OMBASI puts the lighter in his hand. FATHER throws it on the ground.*) No! The spark plug! (*OMBASI shrugs his shoulders, picks up the lighter and puts it away.*)

MOTHER: He's keeping the lighter!

FATHER (*To the BOY*): And why are you crying?

BOY (*Between sobs*): Because . . . because . . . you called me . . . ass . . . hole.

FATHER: When?

BOY: Be . . . before.

FATHER: And, so what? It's nothing to cry about. My father used to call me that all the time, and I turned out alright.

OMBASI: Are we going somewhere? What are you looking for?

FATHER: Look, Sánchez-Vicario, I've had about enough of your shit. Why don't you get out of here? This is all your fault!

OMBASI: *Sánchez-Vicario! Viva España!*

FATHER: It's not funny anymore. The first time, fine, but now it's not funny. Get out of here! Go on! Get out of here!

(*OMBASI takes a few steps away and observes FATHER and the BOY searching in the sand. Then, silently, HE leaves.*)

LITTLE GIRL: How come he always says the same thing?

MOTHER: Maybe because he doesn't know how to say anything else.

LITTLE GIRL: He doesn't know how to say anything else?

MOTHER: No.

LITTLE GIRL: Why?

MOTHER: Because those black people are very uncivilized.

LITTLE GIRL: When can we go?

MOTHER: In a little bit, sweetie. (*SHE hugs the LITTLE GIRL, and with a trace of anguish, looks around. To FATHER.*) It's almost dark.

FATHER: I know. Damn.

LITTLE GIRL: Why aren't we going?

BOY: I can't see.

FATHER: That's no surprise. It's almost dark. What about the lighter?

MOTHER: The black guy took it.

FATHER: What do you mean the black guy took it?

MOTHER: You said it didn't matter.

FATHER: But, how could it not matter? Where is the . . .?

MOTHER: I already told you the black guy took it.

FATHER: I mean the black guy. Where is he?

MOTHER: He left.

FATHER: With my lighter! The bastard left with my lighter?

MOTHER: Because you told him to! He turned around and left!

FATHER: Could he really be such a bastard? Even after I gave him a sandwich!

BOY: It was mine.

FATHER: You, shut up!

FATHER: Where did he go!

MOTHER: I don't know, I don't see him.

LITTLE GIRL: Because he's so black . . .

FATHER: Goddamn it! What are we going to do?

MOTHER: Let's go to the car.

FATHER: For what? We don't have the spark plug!

MOTHER: You idiot! Who would ever think to take out the spark plug?

BOY: What's a spark plug?

MOTHER: Something your father takes out of the car and gives to black men.

FATHER: Very funny!

LITTLE GIRL: Let's go home!

MOTHER: Be quiet, honey. Don't whine, we're looking for the spark plug.

BOY: What if the black man took it?

FATHER: Why would he have taken it?

MOTHER: Didn't he take the lighter?

FATHER: But, why would he want the spark plug?

MOTHER: Maybe he liked it. Maybe he thinks it's one of those magic charms. You know how those people are so primitive . . .

FATHER: Don't say such nonsense.

(Night has fallen.)

4. BEHIND THE DUNE

OMBASI has started a campfire. He has collected branches from bushes and formed a pile, with which he fuels the flame from time to time. The nude BODY of his dead friend lies in a more fitting position, his hands crossed. OMBASI covers him with sand while quietly singing a hymn that suggests a land far, far away. Before covering his friend's head, OMBASI kisses his forehead, eyes and mouth. He finishes covering the BODY and throws into the fire what are presumably small personal items of the dead man. Then, seated on the ground, OMBASI places his head between his knees. He remembers. We hear the sound of his memories.

5. OMBASI'S MEMORIES

With the sound of African tribal music, we hear voices and sounds that reconstruct OMBASI and his friend's voyage.

VOICES IN SEVERAL LANGUAGES *(A mixture of Spanish, French and Arabic)*: Fifteen thousand to go to Tarifa . . . We're leaving, tonight . . . come on, black man. Get on or you're staying here . . . *(Pause. Sound of sea, waves, wind, thunder.)* There are too many of you *(Pause.)* . . . throw out everything you have *(Pause.)* . . . just what we need, the police *(Pause.)* Quiet, okay? We're all on the line here . . . *(Pause.)* Hey, you, stop crying, we're almost there *(Pause.)* . . . in the water *(Pause.)* . . . no, we can't go to shore, they're watching *(Pause.)* Not one word about going back to Morocco! It's great in

Spain. Europe. In the water, I said! We're almost there. You'll swim there in no time. In the water! A bath will do you good!

(Sound of the water grows louder, splashing, panting. Sound of labored breathing. OMBASI pants. HE awakes with a start, with a deep-seated fear in his eyes.)

6. DOWN THE DUNE

The BOY appears on top of the dune. HE peers over cautiously and then speaks, looking back.

BOY: He's here! He's here!
OMBASI: Hello.
FATHER: What?
OMBASI: Hello.
FATHER *(Off stage)*: Wait! Stay back, your mother and I are coming.

(FATHER peers over the top of the dune. OMBASI looks at him and welcomes him with a gesture.)

OMBASI: *Viva España.*
FATHER: Viva España.
BOY: He always says Viva España.
FATHER: He must think it means hello.
BOY: Viva España.

(OMBASI smiles. FATHER descends the dune as HE mutters to the BOY, who follows behind him.)

FATHER:Well, now we have to try not to make him mad and see if he has the spark plug. If he has it, we have to take it from him without him realizing, and then run for it.
BOY: How are we going to take it from him?
OMBASI: Where are your wife and daughter?
MOTHER *(Off stage)*: What's going on? What are you doing? Does he have it?
FATHER *(Shouting)*: I don't know.
OMBASI: You should let her come over. She must be cold.
FATHER: I wonder where the dead guy is?
LITTLE GIRL *(Off stage)*: I'm cold.

OMBASI: Your daughter may be cold. Let her warm up by the fire.

FATHER *(Shouting)*: Stay there! There could be trouble if we have to take the spark plug from him.

MOTHER *(Peering over)*: But Jessie is freezing!

FATHER *(Shouts)*: I said stay there!

OMBASI: You yell at your wife too much. If you don't treat her well, she won't want to sleep with you and it's not the same if you have to force her.

(The BOY moves close to the fire.)

FATHER: What are you doing? Come here!

BOY: Let me stand here a little while. I'm cold.

LITTLE GIRL *(Off stage)*: I'm cold!

MOTHER: Antonio, she's going to catch a cold. Let her at least stand by the fire. Besides, she's half asleep.

LITTLE GIRL *(Peering over)*: I'm cold!

MOTHER *(Descending the slope, to the LITTLE GIRL)*: Alright, sweetie, come on . . .

FATHER: Are you crazy?

MOTHER: Look, Antonio, don't try me! This little girl's going to get pneumonia and this black man has a fire here that I don't even know how he's started *(Pause.)* Well, yes, of course I know how, he did it with that infamous lighter of yours! It seems to me that this black man is smarter than you, seeing as though the only thing you've done is throw away the spark plug, which makes you much more of a savage than him. You hear what I'm telling you!

OMBASI *(To FATHER)*: Your wife likes to yell at you in front of your children. You should beat her with a stick.

LITTLE GIRL *(Shouting)*: Mommy!

MOTHER: Come on, honey.

LITTLE GIRL *(Shaking her head)*: I'm scared of him.

MOTHER: Don't be afraid. He's not going to do anything to you.

LITTLE GIRL: I can't come down with the bucket.

FATHER *(To the BOY)*: Help your sister with the bucket.

BOY *(Who has found a good spot by the fire)*: Aw! Why me? I'm cold.

FATHER *(Begins to strike the BOY in a wild frenzy)*: I said help your sister, damn it, you hear? Don't disobey me! I'm going to, to . . . !

(The BOY screams and runs up the slope crying. As HE passes his MOTHER, SHE caresses him with her hand while glaring reproachfully at her husband. The BOY disappears downhill.)

OMBASI: If you mistreat your son he'll let you to starve to death when you get old.

FATHER *(To OMBASI)*: What are you talking about? Let's see. Spark plug! Do you have the spark plug for my car?

(OMBASI looks at him without understanding.)

MOTHER *(To LITTLE GIRL)*: Go on, honey, go with Daddy and get close to the fire.

LITTLE GIRL: I'm scared.

MOTHER: It's okay, Daddy's there. That man isn't going to do anything to you.

OMBASI *(Smiling at the LITTLE GIRL)*: Hello. *Viva España.*

LITTLE GIRL *(Snuggling closer to her MOTHER)*: He has some really big teeth.

MOTHER: Because he's from the jungle and it's full of wild animals.

FATHER: What sort of crap are you telling her? *(To the LITTLE GIRL.)* Come on, honey, come down here. You're going to catch cold.

MOTHER: We should've gone to the car.

FATHER: And what would we have done in the car? Freeze to death.

MOTHER: It has heat, doesn't it?

FATHER: But we have no battery.

OMBASI: Why don't you tell your family to come over by the fire?

MOTHER: Come on, Jessie. Climb down, honey.

(The LITTLE GIRL shakes her head.)

FATHER: What's wrong with her now?

MOTHER: Come on, don't be silly, Jessie.

LITTLE GIRL: You come with me.

MOTHER: Okay, let's wait for your brother and the three of us will go down together. Ivan!

BOY *(Off stage)*: I'm coming! I dropped the bucket!

MOTHER: What did you drop? Goodness, this boy doesn't have any sense at all! He dropped all the clams!

FATHER: Clams?

OMBASI: You should tell your family to come down. *(Gesturing to MOTHER and the LITTLE GIRL.)* Come over where it's warm. It's cold out!

MOTHER *(To the BOY)*: Hurry and finish picking up those clams or I'm going to tan your hide!

BOY: But the bucket was really heavy.

MOTHER: Really heavy, eh . . . Your father will see about that.

FATHER: Alright, come on, bring her down. Hopefully he has the spark plug and we can leave. Spark plug! It looks like this . . . Small.

MOTHER *(To the LITTLE GIRL)*: Go on, climb down, don't just stand there.

LITTLE GIRL: No. You first. I'm scared.

FATHER: Shut up! No one can understand with all this racket!

(LITTLE GIRL sneezes.)

OMBASI: Your daughter is going to catch cold.

MOTHER: Oh no, now she's going to get a cold. Climb down, damn it! *(Obstinately, the LITTLE GIRL shakes her head.)* We'll see how you feel when you get pneumonia!

FATHER *(To OMBASI)*: Look, if you have the spark plug, give it to me and I'll give you something else you might like. It won't do you any good. I'll give you money for it.

MOTHER: Why give him money if it's yours?

FATHER: Hell, be quiet. He doesn't have it. It fell out of my pocket!

OMBASI *(Showing him the lighter, he holds it out to him)*: Here. You might need it.

FATHER: No, not this.

MOTHER: So what? Take it! It's yours, isn't it?

(FATHER takes the lighter that OMBASI hands him. The BOY peers over with the bucket.)

BOY: Help me, I can't make it with the bucket!

MOTHER *(Looks inside the bucket)*: Are these all the clams that are left? *(Pinching the BOY.)* Are these all the clams that are left!

BOY *(Squirming about)*: You should've gone to get it!

FATHER: What? Is that how you talk to your mother!

(Furious, FATHER clumsily begins scaling the side of the dune to reach his son, but falls halfway up and slides back down, almost falling into the fire. HE even manages to push OMBASI, who almost burns himself. OMBASI falls on top of the sand covered BODY. OMBASI gets up and screams.)

FATHER *(To the BOY)*: Goddamn it! I'm going to skin you alive!

OMBASI *(Angrily, to FATHER)*: Enough already, alright! Could you stop yelling! You almost threw me in the fire!

(The whole FAMILY is frightened.)

MOTHER: He's angry.

LITTLE GIRL: Let's go home! I don't like it here!

FATHER *(Lying on the ground at OMBASI'S feet, frightened by his angry expression)*: Now, now. Take it easy. We're leaving. Easy.

OMBASI: Tell your family to come down, don't be selfish, let them warm up, too.

FATHER: Alright, alright, we're leaving. *(To his FAMILY.)* As soon as we find the police this bastard is going to get what's coming to him. Let's go before things get any worse.

OMBASI *(Stretching his arms upward and speaking to the LITTLE GIRL)*: Come, little one, come on down. I'll catch you. Don't pay your father any mind. He's crazy.

FATHER *(Starting to climb the dune)*: Let's go. He'll get his. Who knows what he's doing here. He's going to be in for it.

LITTLE GIRL: Why is he gonna be in for it?

BOY: I want to come down. I'm cold. I got wet from the water in the bucket.

FATHER: You're going to do what I tell you. And you're going to get it when this is all over.

BOY: I'm staying here with the black man.

LITTLE GIRL *(Crying hysterically)*: Don't stay! He's going to kill you just like he killed the other black man!

FATHER: Let him stay if he wants, because if not, I'll be the one who kills him.

MOTHER: Are you crazy? You're going to let Ivan stay? What if he does something to him?

FATHER *(Still climbing)*: Look, dammit! Weren't you the one who said . . .?

(The BOY, on his very own, descends the side of the slope, dragging the bucket with him.)

MOTHER: Ivan!

BOY *(To OMBASI)*: Hello, Sánchez-Vicario.

OMBASI: *Viva España.* Your family is leaving?

BOY *(Moving closer to the fire)*: It's so cold!

MOTHER: Ivan! Come up here right now!

BOY: I don't want to.

FATHER: I said come up here!

BOY: No.

OMBASI: Why don't you all just come down? The fire needs more wood. There's some brush growing back there.

BOY: Where's the dead man that was with you?

OMBASI: If you have food, we can eat. *(Making a customary eating gesture.)*

BOY *(Half fearful and fascinated)*: You ate him?

LITTLE GIRL: He ate the other black man!

MOTHER: Be quiet, Jessie. God, you're driving me crazy!

OMBASI: Are you going to come down?

MOTHER: What do we do? She's cold and she's going to get sick.

FATHER: Alright, we'll go down, slowly, no yelling. *(To the BOY, in a low voice, so as not to alarm OMBASI.)* And you're going to keep quiet or I'm going to rearrange your face, do you hear me, nitwit? Now we're all going to go down together, slowly . . . Come here, Jessie. *(Holding out his arms to the LITTLE GIRL, who doesn't want to let go of her MOTHER.)*

MOTHER: Go on, honey, go with Daddy. I'm coming, too.

LITTLE GIRL: What if he eats me?

MOTHER: He won't eat you. He's a good guy.

LITTLE GIRL: No! He's bad! He eats people!

MOTHER: Okay, but he's not hungry right now.

FATHER: Would you please stop filling her head with that nonsense!

OMBASI *(Holding out his arms toward the LITTLE GIRL again)*: Come on, come down. You, too, Ma'am.

(FATHER, MOTHER and LITTLE GIRL fumble down the slope. OMBASI smiles. The LITTLE GIRL keeps her distance from him and looks at him suspiciously.)

BOY: He's laughing.

FATHER: Well, I don't know what the bastard has to laugh about.

MOTHER: Well, because thanks to your lighter he's started a fire and has been nice and toasty for an hour now, while we've been here acting the fool. Why else?

(The BOY watches OMBASI laugh and laughs as well. FATHER, MOTHER and LITTLE GIRL form a small distrustful group facing OMBASI, who sits beside the fire and looks at them. The BOY sits next to him. OMBASI peers into the bucket of clams.)

OMBASI: May I eat some of these?

BOY: Daddy, he's going to eat the clams.

LITTLE GIRL: You see? He is bad. He wants to eat all of our clams.

OMBASI: Sit. Let's eat them.

MOTHER: She's cold.

FATHER: She should go over by the fire.

LITTLE GIRL: You come with me.

(FATHER and the LITTLE GIRL sit alongside the fire. The LITTLE GIRL curls up beside him. Afterwards, MOTHER and BOY do the same. OMBASI tosses a few branches on the fire. Then HE points to the bucket of clams.)

OMBASI: Can we eat these?

(OMBASI removes a knife from his pocket. FATHER and MOTHER, restless, exchange glances, yet they don't find OMBASI'S gestures threatening. OMBASI takes a clam out of the bucket and opens it. HE offers it to the LITTLE GIRL, who makes a gesture of repulsion.)

LITTLE GIRL: Mommy! He wants me to eat a raw clam!
MOTHER: No, honey. Come here.

(The LITTLE GIRL hides in her mother's arms.)

FATHER: It's okay, you can eat them.

(OMBASI offers it to the FATHER, who accepts after slight hesitation.)

MOTHER: What are you doing?
FATHER: What? They're ours. We caught them.
MOTHER: Yeah, but . . .

(OMBASI hands the knife to MOTHER, and points to the bucket of clams, and then points to those present.)

MOTHER: What does he want?
FATHER: He's giving it to you so you can eat if you want.
MOTHER: No, no, I don't want any.
FATHER: Kids, you want some clams?
BOY: Not me. Gross. They're raw.
FATHER: Does she want some?
MOTHER: She's fallen asleep.
FATHER: She may get cold.
OMBASI: Maybe she is cold.

(OMBASI picks up an article of clothing that he took from the DEAD MAN and goes over to the LITTLE GIRL to cover her with it. The MOTHER becomes anxious.)

FATHER: It's okay, don't worry. He's just covering her. *(To OMBASI.)* Thank you.

MOTHER *(Covering the LITTLE GIRL more completely)*: Couldn't that old jacket have fleas?

FATHER: What's with you! Why would it have fleas? When he's not looking, see if the spark plug is in the pocket.

(OMBASI eats clams. MOTHER searches carefully. SHE shakes her head in negative response.)

BOY: He's eating all the clams.

FATHER *(To OMBASI)*: Hey, you, smart guy, let me hold the knife. *(Holds out his hand. OMBASI gives it to him. To MOTHER.)* Do you want some?

MOTHER: It gives me the creeps. What if the knife has AIDS on it or something?

FATHER: Why would it have AIDS? Damn, now you've made me nervous. *(To the BOY.)* Hey, you! Don't eat them. *(FATHER returns the knife to OMBASI.)*

BOY: I wasn't going to eat them. They're gross raw.

(THEY remain quiet as OMBASI continues to eat clams, apparently enjoying them.)

FATHER: Well, the knife might have AIDS, but damn if he's not getting a belly full.

OMBASI: They're good. In my country we catch bigger ones, we call them clams, and then there are oysters that are even bigger, but you have to dive for them. My friend was very good at digging them up. And he was a good swimmer, but . . .

7. BEHIND THE DUNE

OMBASI continues talking. While OMBASI speaks, the BOY has fallen asleep, curled up beside him. FATHER nods off sleepily and MOTHER watches OMBASI speak without understanding him, yet nodding her head courteously. Realizing that FATHER is sleeping, SHE elbows him and HE awakens startled, instantly nodding off again.

OMBASI: He got a cramp when we were approaching the shore. I dragged him, but he was so heavy. We were both sinking. They told us we were close, but it seemed like we'd never get there. It was raining; it was dark; you couldn't see anything. Do you want to see him? Well, maybe it's better if you don't. He was going to marry my sister when we got back, but now that he's dead, my sister will have to marry his brother. It won't be the same. His brother likes to hit women, even if they haven't done anything. You don't understand me, do you?

(MOTHER looks at him expressionless and smiles. OMBASI smiles. MOTHER looks anxiously at her husband. Finally, OMBASI tiredly places his head between his bent knees.)

MOTHER *(To FATHER)*: You're sleeping.
FATHER: Hell, I had to get up at six this morning to check the car.
MOTHER: Why did we have to come so far?
FATHER: Because there are no clams left anywhere else.
MOTHER: Don't go to sleep.
FATHER: I'm sleepy.
MOTHER: It doesn't matter. Don't go to sleep.
FATHER: Why?
MOTHER: I'm scared.
FATHER: Of what?
MOTHER: Everything. Him.
FATHER: He's asleep. You should sleep, too.
MOTHER: I can only sleep in my own bed, you know that. Besides, my back hurts. I don't like sleeping away from home.
FATHER: What about when we're on vacation?
MOTHER: You know I don't get a wink of sleep the whole two weeks. Besides, no one sleeps when you go camping. Between the mosquitoes, the people in the other tents, and getting up to make sure the kids aren't tangled in their sleeping bags, I'm up the whole night. I can't stand camping. I'm afraid the kids are going to suffocate in their sleeping bags, the showers gross me out,

the sink, the water, everything. But what really repulses me is the bathroom. I don't go for a whole week because I'm so disgusted.

FATHER: Well, you said you liked it.

MOTHER: So you wouldn't get upset.

FATHER: So why are you telling me now?

MOTHER: Because today nothing matters to me. It's like today doesn't count.

FATHER: You say the strangest things. Try to sleep, okay.

MOTHER: I can't. My back hurts. Besides, he scares me. What if he does something to us?

FATHER: I don't think so. I'm watching him.

MOTHER: You? You'll be asleep as soon as I close my eyes.

FATHER: Well, so what? I'm tired.

MOTHER: I'm tired, too. What do you think?

FATHER: Nothing, woman, I don't mean anything by it. I'm just saying that I'm tired and I'd like you to go to sleep.

MOTHER: If you're the tired one, why don't you go to sleep?

FATHER: Shhhh! You're going to wake the kids.

MOTHER: I don't like that Ivan is lying so close to him. Maybe he has lice *(Pause.)* or ringworm, I think they get it a lot in those countries. Even leprosy.

FATHER *(Leaning back, almost asleep)*: No.

MOTHER: And what do you know?

FATHER: Go to sleep.

MOTHER: I can't, my back hurts.

FATHER: If you go to sleep you won't feel it.

MOTHER: I don't see how you can sleep so easily!

FATHER: I'm tired. First thing tomorrow we'll go out to the highway to see if someone comes by.

MOTHER: I don't know why we came so far.

FATHER: Because we wanted to get clams. Go to sleep.

MOTHER: And if he wakes up and does something to us?

FATHER: I'll keep watch.

MOTHER: You? You're half asleep.

FATHER: I sleep with one eye open, you know that.

MOTHER: Since when? When the kids would cry, you never knew about it. Remember when Ivan was sick with that ear infection, you didn't even realize it and I was up the whole night.

FATHER: Because I had to go to work.

MOTHER: But you didn't even hear him.

FATHER: Yes, I did, but I couldn't get up. Go on, go to sleep. *(As if giving in to an old habit, and on the verge of falling asleep, HE puts his hand between his wife's thighs. SHE shivers.)*

MOTHER: Be still. Can't you tell that he can see us?

FATHER: Mmmmmm. *(Leaves his hand where it is and sleeps.)*

MOTHER: Antonio.

FATHER: Mmmmm.

MOTHER: Antonio, don't fall asleep.

FATHER: I'm not.

MOTHER: You were sleeping.

FATHER: No, I wasn't.

MOTHER: You're not fooling me. You were sleeping. Your whole family is in danger and you're sleeping.

FATHER: I'm not sleeping.

(OMBASI changes his posture to get more comfortable. MOTHER shivers. FATHER is startled and sits up, alarmed. OMBASI sleeps.)

MOTHER: You scared me.

FATHER: And you scared me. You see? He's asleep.

MOTHER: Where could he have come from?

FATHER: I don't know . . . from Africa.

MOTHER: As soon as it's daylight, we're going and leaving him here. I don't ever want to see him again.

FATHER: Why? He hasn't done anything to us.

MOTHER: It's all his fault. We were just fine until he showed up. What could he have come for?

FATHER: How do I know? To look for work.

MOTHER: You see. Since there's no work here . . . they all get mixed up with drugs eventually. We have to tell the police.

FATHER: Stay out of it. We're going to leave and, good riddance, as if we never saw him.

MOTHER *(Motioning that she is in pain)*: My back hurts more and more. Promise me we won't go camping this year.

FATHER: But the kids like it.

MOTHER: Well, I don't.

FATHER: So what do you want to do? Stay home?

MOTHER: I'd prefer to.

FATHER: And how come you've suddenly got something against camping?

MOTHER: I don't know. Because it came to mind. I've had some strange thoughts today.

FATHER: Alright, go to sleep. I'll keep watch.

MOTHER: I can't.

FATHER: Try.

MOTHER: God, my back hurts. Ever since she was born it's been like this.
FATHER: Go to sleep . . .

8. DREAMS

Some time has passed. Everyone sleeps. The fire has gone out. Stars are shining, waves are breaking.

OMBASI suddenly opens his eyes and stares at the sleeping woman. The WOMAN awakens, shaken, and looks at him. THEY look at each other for a moment. OMBASI crawling, approaches her. When he reaches her, HE raises her skirt. SHE watches as he does so, terrified, but does not resist. OMBASI caresses her and kisses her thighs. MOTHER opens her mouth to a silent scream. SHE looks at her husband and shakes him in a vain attempt to wake him up.

Short blackout. When the lights come up, THEY are back in their positions. The WOMAN awakens, shaken, and looks at her surroundings. SHE looks at OMBASI, who sleeps fitfully. SHE sighs and watches her children sleeping tranquilly. SHE moves close to her husband, seeking protection. FATHER mutters in his dreams and once again places his hands between her legs, and SHE caresses the LITTLE GIRL'S head and closes her eyes.

Then, the friend's lifeless BODY stirs. HE sits up, shaking away the sand. The BODY is naked. OMBASI opens his eyes.

OMBASI: What are you doing here?
BODY: Nothing. I'm not doing anything. Not here or anywhere else. I don't have to do anything. But you do. You'll have to do something. What are you going to do?
OMBASI: I don't know. I'm really tired.
BODY: The bugs are starting to bite me all over. Those white ones.
OMBASI: I don't know what they do with the dead in this country.
BODY: Those children think you killed me. Their parents don't know I'm here.
OMBASI: They're really strange people. They're so frightened and they yell at each other.
BODY: They're scared. And far from home.
OMBASI: I'm further away from mine.
BODY: You don't have a home.
OMBASI: I'll have one. Two. One here and another one there.
BODY: Maybe not. Neither here nor there. You won't want to go back because you don't have anything there, but you won't have anything here either, and you'll be neither here nor there. Be careful. It gets cold here in the winter. And in the gray cities, colder yet.

OMBASI: I won't go out. I'll stay warm in my house.

BODY: You won't have a house. Or maybe you will, one like mine, cold and wet. These white bugs bite hard.

OMBASI: I'll have a brick house, with lights on the ceiling and a tile floor.

BODY: You won't, Ombasi. I've known many that came before us.

OMBASI: But you've only known the dead ones, the ones that failed.

BODY: Don't be fooled. They fooled us enough during the trip.

OMBASI: It's the Moroccans' fault. We lost everything there.

BODY: It'll be worse here. Here, they don't like us. Nor do they even care enough to rob us. They think we've come to take what's theirs. Even if we settle for what they don't want, it doesn't matter. They think we pollute the stinking air they breathe. You've seen these people. They acted like you were going to kill them. The woman dreamed you were going to rape her.

OMBASI: Dreams come and go. It's no one's fault. If we didn't dream, we'd go crazy. Even dogs dream, don't they? They move their paws and growl.

BODY: But if that man knew what his wife was dreaming, he'd probably kill you. He'd blame you.

OMBASI: That I understand. I would do the same. She's his wife, even if they both are dreaming.

BODY: Well, that makes no sense.

OMBASI: It also made no sense for you to drown just when we were about to get here.

BODY: You'll drown, too.

OMBASI: I don't intend to go near that water again.

BODY: You won't need to. You'll drown in misery and illness, in dirt and pis.

OMBASI: How do you know?

BODY: I've seen it. They told me. You'll sleep underground, still alive, smelling like urine, and every passerby will turn away from you. Some will laugh at you, some will despise you, some will humiliate you, some will hit you, others will be afraid of you, and those that think they're better than you will pity you. I've seen it, they've told me.

OMBASI: Because you only talk to the ones who are bitter and who've failed. Here there are doctors, more than enough food, and children don't die with flies in their eyes. You can do business. *(The BODY takes a water-filled bowl, we's his fingers and sprinkles OMBASI.)* What are you doing? Why are you putting water on me?

BODY: You're going to have problems, brother.

OMBASI: And you'll have them, too, if you don't stop putting water on me. You're an idiot. I don't know what my sister saw in you. I shouldn't have brought you.

BODY: You want me to tell you what's going to happen to your sister with my brother?

OMBASI: Your brother is another blockhead just like you, but worse. You were a fool for drowning.

BODY: My shoes were really heavy. And the bag tied to my neck didn't help.

OMBASI: Why didn't you take them off like I did? Stop sprinkling water on me! Who would ever think of swimming with shoes on?

BODY: But now you've put them on. And you're keeping my things.

OMBASI: You don't need them anymore! What do you want shoes for, huh?

BODY: You'll drown with them.

OMBASI: Get out of here! And stop throwing water on me.

BODY: I'm not the one throwing water on you. Don't you see it's raining?

(Brief blackout.)

9. BEHIND THE DUNE

Morning. When the lights come up, the family stirs. MOTHER covers the LITTLE GIRL. OMBASI opens his eyes in wonder.

FATHER: Goddamn it! Now it's raining! *(To the BOY.)* Hey, you! Wake up, it's raining. My back is going to be so sore tonight.

BOY: It's raining!

FATHER: That's what I'm trying to tell you!

MOTHER: Put something over you! You're going to catch cold, that's the last thing we need.

LITTLE GIRL: It's raining! It's raining!

BOY: We already know, Jessie!

MOTHER: We should've gone to the car. We're going to get soaked. Just what Ivan needs with his ear problems.

FATHER: Well, it's only drizzling. Don't exaggerate.

OMBASI: It's raining. We should go inside somewhere.

MOTHER: Do you hear me? We should've gone to the car!

FATHER: What would we have done in the car?

MOTHER: More than what we would do out here.

OMBASI: Why don't we go to your house? You have a house, don't you? A brick one.

BOY *(To OMBASI)*: What did you say?

FATHER: Look, Sánchez-Vicario is up.

OMBASI: Viva España.

FATHER: Oh, God. He's at it again.

LITTLE GIRL: Look, he's getting wet.

MOTHER: Stop looking at him. He might want to come with us.

LITTLE GIRL: Is he coming with us?

MOTHER: Shhhh! Be quiet! He can't.

LITTLE GIRL: He's getting wet. Is his color going to wash off?

MOTHER: No, it won't wash off.

LITTLE GIRL: Where's his house?

MOTHER: We'll look for it later on the map.

FATHER: Come on, now let's see if we can find the spark plug where I dropped it last night.

MOTHER: You didn't drop it. You threw it away.

FATHER: Alright, fine, but don't bust my balls about it now.

(The CHILDREN, awestruck, stand looking at the father.)

LITTLE GIRL: What are balls?

(The BOY bursts into a contagious laughter that infects OMBASI.)

FATHER: What is this asshole laughing about now?

MOTHER: It's not his fault. He sees Ivan laughing and—

FATHER: I don't mean him, I mean your son, who is just like everyone in your family.

BOY: I was laughing at what Jessie said.

LITTLE GIRL *(To OMBASI)*: You're gonna get wet. He's gonna get wet, Mommy. What if he gets a sore throat?

MOTHER: Don't worry. He'll go somewhere.

BOY: Right! Where's he gonna go?

MOTHER: I don't know. He'll go somewhere.

BOY: We can take him some place.

FATHER: Great, just what we needed. Come on, let's all look for the spark plug. Come on. Let's go.

MOTHER: I don't know, maybe if we take him to the Red Cross . . .

FATHER: Look, he should be grateful I haven't called the police. Come on, we're going to end up getting soaked in this drizzling rain.

LITTLE GIRL: I want to pee pee.

MOTHER: Well, go pee pee over there.

(The LITTLE GIRL climbs the mound where the BODY is buried and takes down her panties, getting ready to pee. When OMBASI realizes, he rushes

over to her, lifting her into the air and carrying her to another spot. The LITTLE GIRL shrieks in fear with her behind in the air and her legs flailing.)

OMBASI: No, no, child, you can't pee on the grave, because then my dead friend will get up and smack you on your little bottom!

FATHER *(Seeing what OMBASI is doing, throws himself on him)*: What are you doing to my daughter, you black bastard!

MOTHER *(Shouting)*: Oh, my Jessie! What is he doing to my Jessie?

(OMBASI raises his arms to defend himself from the attack. The LITTLE GIRL falls on her behind. SHE cries. MOTHER runs over and drags her away. The LITTLE GIRL cries, peeing at the same time. FATHER confronts OMBASI.)

FATHER: You touch my daughter again, and I swear I'll kill you! You hear!
(HE pushes OMBASI who falls on top of his friend's tomb. Amazed, OMBASI looks at the father.)

OMBASI: Hey, you, what's the matter. I was only keeping your daughter from pissing on my friend.

FATHER: Stay back! Let's get out of here. This guy is an animal.

MOTHER *(To the BOY)*: What are you looking at? Let's go.

BOY: I'm looking at the dead man.

(The BODY's black foot sticks out beside OMBASI.)

MOTHER: Stop that nonsense!

FATHER: It's true. Look.

(Mesmerized, the FAMILY look at the foot emerging from the sand. OMBASI, who hasn't noticed the foot of the body, is frightened as he feels himself being watched.)

LITTLE GIRL: Let's go home!

FATHER: This is worse than I thought. The son of a bitch has buried a dead man.

MOTHER: Let's go to the car, Antonio, please. When it stops raining, we'll look for the spark plug. But let's go. Even if we have to walk.

(Sound of distant thunder.)

OMBASI: It's going to storm. Let's run.

(OMBASI gets up. Afraid, the FAMILY take steps backward.)

FATHER: Stay away from my family, you got it? Let's go. Climb on up. I'll keep him busy.

(THEY start to climb the dune. MOTHER goes first with the LITTLE GIRL, then, the BOY follows.)

BOY: What about the clams?

FATHER: Let him keep them, maybe he'll get sick from them.

LITTLE GIRL: My shovel! I want my shovel!

MOTHER: We'll buy you another one later. Let's go, we're getting wet.

OMBASI: Are you leaving? Can I go with you? I'm cold.

FATHER: I said don't move! You'll see when the police get here. You'll be in for it.

(MOTHER and CHILDREN disappear behind the dune. OMBASI stares at FATHER.)

OMBASI: Can I go with you? Can you take me somewhere I can work?

FATHER: I'm going up. Careful what you do. Stay put.

OMBASI: Thank you. I'll follow you. I won't bother you. I only need a tiny bit of space.

(FATHER begins climbing the side of the dune. OMBASI watches him and starts to follow behind him.)

FATHER: What are you doing? I said don't come up!

OMBASI: I can work. I'm strong. I can help you in your brick house, I'll clean your tile floor, shine your light fixtures.

FATHER *(Approaching the top of the dune)*: I'm telling you for the last time. You can't come.

(OMBASI attempts to climb up again and FATHER tries to push him down with his foot, but HE misses and falls downhill. HE lands at OMBASI's feet, his mouth full of sand.)

OMBASI: Not only are you stupid, you're clumsy, too.

FATHER: Take your hands off me! Damn it, I hurt myself. *(Spits sand.)* All your fault! *(Sound of thunder.)* It's raining harder and harder and we're here with this kaffir.

(OMBASI collects the items that FATHER has dropped.)

OMBASI: You dropped your things again. Here, this is yours. *(Handing him his things. OMBASI helps him to his feet and brushes sand from FATHER's clothing.)*

FATHER: Give it here. And leave once and for all. You've already screwed me up enough. Somebody should keep an eye on you. Is this your dead man?

OMBASI *(Turning, he sees his friend's foot)*: My friend. He drowned. They brought us in a boat, with a motor, put-put-put ... some fishermen took us to some Moroccans. There, they took all our money. Then they threw us in the water. My friend drowned. He didn't take off his shoes. These shoes. They're big on me. See? He's bigger than I am. Look at those feet. Do you want to see him? *(Making a gesture as if to dig up the body. FATHER winces in disgust.)*

FATHER: What are you doing? Don't move!

OMBASI: You don't want to see him? He was my friend. I don't know what to do with him. I'm going to leave him here. He won't care, right? I want to go with you and your family. Then I'll go, work and come back.

FATHER: Alright, alright, that's enough. I don't want to hear your life story. *(Thrusting the items into his pocket. HE then touches something hard on the inside. He looks through the lining of his jacket.)* Dammit! There's a hole in my pocket . . . *(Forcing the spark plug from the lining.)* The spark plug! The damn spark plug! *(Euphorically holding it up high.)*

OMBASI: What is that? It's for your car, right? Vrrrmm!

BOY *(Off stage)*: Daddy!

MOTHER *(Off stage)*: Antonio! Is something wrong?

BOY *(Peering over the crest of the dune)*: Can we go now?

FATHER: Yeah, we're going. Tell your mother I found the spark plug.

BOY: Is the dead man still there?

FATHER: Of course he's still here, you idiot! Where's he gonna go!

(The BOY disappears behind the dune.)

BOY *(Off stage)*: Mom! Dad found the spark plug!

FATHER: Okay, I'm leaving. You stay here. Don't even think about following me. *(FATHER begins to climb.)*

OMBASI: I'm coming with you.

FATHER: You better go back to the jungle because here you're just a fish out of water. Dammit to hell! I hurt myself!

(FATHER disappears. OMBASI stands still, staring at the place where he disappeared.)

OMBASI *(Addressing the tomb)*: I have to leave you here. You don't mind, do you? I'm going with them. I'm taking your things. Goodbye, brother. I'm sorry you drowned. I dreamed about you. Well, I'm leaving. I can't stay here. They're taking me in their car. *(OMBASI covers the body's foot and carefully smoothes a bit of the sand on the tomb. Then HE collects the things scattered about, including the bucket of clams. HE prepares to climb the dune, but before doing so, returns the bucket to the ground and urinates for a long moment in a corner. HE speaks while urinating.)* And another thing: If you see my father, tell him not to be upset that I haven't thought about him much. But tell him that what happened to him wasn't my fault. I didn't know he was going to die from coughing. Everybody coughs, right? I let him have my bed. But I think he died angry with me. He looked at me as if I was the one who killed him and that wasn't so. He got sick, started coughing and then died. That doesn't happen here. If you cough, they take you to a hospital, and they take care of you. Well, I'm leaving. *(HE starts climbing the dune. Sound of thunder.)*

10. THE BEACH

The FAMILY moves along, walking through the sand.

FATHER: At least it has stopped raining.
MOTHER: For now. Where's the car?
FATHER: It can't be too far.
BOY: Where's the car, Dad?
FATHER: It's close by.
LITTLE GIRL: I want to go to the car.
MOTHER: And to think . . . it was in your pocket.
FATHER: My jacket was torn and it fell through the lining.
MOTHER: How come you didn't look carefully in your pocket?
FATHER: I did look carefully.
MOTHER: Yeah, so I see.
FATHER: If you took better care of my clothes this wouldn't have happened!
MOTHER: Everybody must be looking for us. Surely my mother called the police.
FATHER: Your mother doesn't even know.
MOTHER: What a night, all because of your infamous spark plug. And where the hell did you leave the car?
FATHER: Don't talk like that in front of the kids.
LITTLE GIRL: I want breakfast.
BOY: Where's the car?

FATHER: I said we're almost there, dammit!

(A flash of lightning. The LITTLE GIRL screams.)

LITTLE GIRL: Mommy! It's lightning!
MOTHER: It's okay. Let's say a rhyme: "Rain, rain, go away . . . come again another day."
FATHER: What kind of nonsense is that?
MOTHER: I don't know how it goes and it doesn't matter. It's the thought that counts, right?
BOY: I think the car was the other way.
FATHER: What did you say?
BOY: We left the car on the other side.
LITTLE GIRL: How does it go?
MOTHER: Hush now, honey.
FATHER *(To the BOY)*: What did you say?
BOY: I said, I think the sea was on that side of us.
FATHER: Nonsense. *(But, HE looks both ways, disoriented.)*
MOTHER: We are going the right way, aren't we?
FATHER: I don't know. Your son has me just as lost as he is.
MOTHER: Don't get confused. It was over there. We're going the right way.
BOY: No.
FATHER: Yes, we are. Your mother and I say it was over there, alright? Who knows better?
BOY *(Shrugging his shoulders)*: Fine, but I don't think so.
FATHER: You be quiet! You're always confusing people!
LITTLE GIRL: I'm hungry.
MOTHER: There should be a piece of peanut butter sandwich left from yesterday.

(MOTHER searches in her bag and takes out half a sandwich.)

LITTLE GIRL: I don't want it. Someone bit off it.

(MOTHER, suddenly rushes over to the LITTLE GIRL and slaps her.)

MOTHER *(Hysterically)*: Well, you're going to eat it! There's nothing else, you stupid! You're going to eat it! Eat it! Eat it! *(Letting go of the LITTLE GIRL, screaming and in tears.)* I want to go home! Where's the car? *(To FATHER.)* Where is the car, you bastard! You idiot! Where is the car, you idiot? You're worse than an idiot! You had the spark plug in your pocket the whole time and had us all sleeping out in the open with that black man who could've killed us and almost disgraced our little girl!

(Terrified, the CHILDREN look at their MOTHER. The LITTLE GIRL begins to cry.)

FATHER: Take it easy, don't get like that. It's alright, we're going to the car and in a little while we'll be home . . . Calm down.

MOTHER: Calm down? I've been trying to calm down since yesterday. I didn't want to go! I wanted to stay home and watch a video. My back was hurting, but you just had to come out here . . . driving 100 miles to catch clams for your boss, asshole . . . you are an asshole!

FATHER: Alright, that's enough. Would you be quiet?

MOTHER: I don't want to, you ass!

FATHER: I'm warning you Dori. If you insult me again . . .

MOTHER: What, asshole?

FATHER: Goddamn it, Dori! I said don't insult me!

(HE tries to reach her, but she escapes. THEY chase each other in the sand. The CHILDREN cry. MOTHER trips and falls. FATHER rushes at her, raising his hand to hit her.)

MOTHER: Kids! Look! Look at your father! Look, how dare he! With me of all people! With me, you see!

BOY *(Hurling himself at FATHER)*: No! Leave her alone, Dad!

(FATHER stops and sobs over the MOTHER, both on the ground.)

LITTLE GIRL *(Crying)*: No, Daddy, look, I'm eating the peanut butter, see? I'm eating the peanut butter! *(SHE nibbles on the sandwich and then drops it. She recovers it, shakes off the sand and continues eating it.)* I'm eating it, see? I'm eating it!

(MOTHER stands and caresses the LITTLE GIRL.)

MOTHER: It's okay, honey . . . Let's go, before the rain starts again. *(To the BOY.)* Let's go.

BOY: I think it was on the other side.

FATHER: Everything was that black guy's fault. If he hadn't shown up!

OMBASI *(Off stage)*: Hey! Heeeey!

(EVERYONE turns around.)

MOTHER: It's him! It's him! My God, it's him! What does he want now?
LITTLE GIRL: Mommy! It's the black man!
BOY: But, why is he coming again?
FATHER: He couldn't be such a bastard, could he? Let's go!

(EVERYONE runs off.)

11. A PLACE ON THE BEACH

EVERYONE runs on stage. FATHER carries the LITTLE GIRL in his arms.

FATHER: Let's go, run!

> *(THEY cross the scene. After a few moments, OMBASI crosses behind them with the bucket of clams.)*

OMBASI: Hey! Heeeey!

12. ANOTHER PLACE ON THE BEACH

Once again, the FAMILY runs on stage.

FATHER: Come on! Come on! The car has to be right here!

> *(The BOY stops.)*

BOY: I can't run anymore! Dad!
FATHER: Come on, try. We're close now. I think I can see the car!

> *(Thunder and lightning. It starts to rain.)*

MOTHER: We have to get there.
BOY *(Falling on the sand)*: I can't.
MOTHER: This is absurd. He's going to catch us. He runs faster than we do. All black people run faster. Haven't you seen the Olympics?
FATHER: Go to the car. I'll talk to him. I'll tell him to leave us alone. We have to get out of here.

(The storm grows violently worse.)

LITTLE GIRL: Mommy! How did the "rain, rain" thing go?
MOTHER: "Rain, rain, go away. If you don't, then we can't play."
LITTLE GIRL: That's not how it went.
FATHER: Get in the car and wait for me there. Take the keys. *(Searching in his pocket.)* Keys . . . keys . . . *(His expression changes.)* The keys!
LITTLE GIRL: Daddy, the black man is coming!
FATHER: Keys.
MOTHER: I have them! *(Removing them from her bag.)*
FATHER: Shit, you should've said something!
MOTHER: I forgot. Come on, kids.
OMBASI *(Off stage)*: Heeey!
FATHER: Come on! To the car!

(MOTHER and CHILDREN head for the car. MOTHER stops and turns to FATHER.)

MOTHER: Be careful.
FATHER: Go on, hurry up!

(MOTHER and CHILDREN go off stage. FATHER stands and waits for OMBASI. OMBASI enters with the bucket of clams.)

OMBASI: Wait! I want to go with you! *Viva España!*
FATHER *(Confronting OMBASI)*: What are you doing here? Huh? What are you doing here? Get out of here! *(Grabbing onto his clothing and shaking him.)* What did you come for? Viva España, eh? Viva España, eh!

(OMBASI falls on the sand with the bucket and everything else, and FATHER runs off after his family.)

13. THE CAR

Inside the car, MOTHER and CHILDREN noisily encourage FATHER.

CHILDREN: Run, Daddy! Runnnnnnn!
MOTHER: Come on, Antonio, for God's sake! Run! Let's get out of here!

> *(THEY ALL shout and weep simultaneously. FATHER reaches them in a mad dash. HE sits at the steering wheel and tries to start the car.)*

MOTHER: What's wrong?
FATHER: The spark plug!
MOTHER: The infamous spark plug!
FATHER: I have to put it in!

> *(FATHER gets out of the car and lifts the hood.)*

BOY: Run, Dad! He's coming!

> *(FATHER pokes around under the hood. OMBASI reaches him. The LITTLE GIRL screams.)*

LITTLE GIRL: He's gonna get you, Daddy! He's gonna get you!
MOTHER: Antonio! Antonioooo!
FATHER *(Confronting OMBASI)*: Get out of here once and for all! Leave me alone! Leave us alone!
OMBASI: Take it easy. I only want you to take me with you. Is something wrong with the car? Take me somewhere.
FATHER *(Slamming the hood)*: Enough already! Get out of here! Leave or I'll kill you!
OMBASI: Take me to your city. I want to work.
FATHER: Get out of here, dammit!
MOTHER: Did you do it?
FATHER: Yes!
MOTHER: Well, let's go!
FATHER: That's what I'm trying to do! But this . . . !
MOTHER: Get in the car and let's go!
FATHER *(To OMBASI)*: Go on, out of here! You hear?
OMBASI: I'm so tired. Take me somewhere.
LITTLE GIRL: Why is he crying?
MOTHER: He's not crying, it just looks like it. Let's go, Antonio!

BOY: Dad, I'll start the car!
MOTHER: Sit still.
BOY: I know how. *(The BOY starts the ignition.)*
OMBASI: Vrrrmmm! It's working. Let's go! When we get to your city, I'll get out.
FATHER: Good job, son! Keep it running, I'm coming right now.

(And in one dash, HE gets into the car and slams the door. OMBASI goes after him.)

OMBASI: Don't go! Take me! I won't do anything to you! I don't want to die out here!
MOTHER: Get out of here!

(OMBASI beats desperately on the car and throws himself on the hood.)

OMBASI: Take me to your city!
MOTHER: Go, go, Antonio! Run over him if you have to!

(Finally, FATHER, howling in rage, gets out of the car with the security bar for the steering wheel.)

FATHER: Enough! Get out of here! Leave us alone!

(HE tries to hit OMBASI, but unfortunately strikes the car instead, breaking the windshield. Everyone inside the car yells.)

MOTHER: My God, Antonio, be careful!
OMBASI: What are you doing? Why are you trying to kill me! I'm not trying to take anything from you, fool! Son of a bitch, don't even think about hitting me!

(FATHER tries to hit him again. OMBASI throws himself on him. THEY fall to the ground. The bar falls.)

MOTHER: Be careful! Remember he had a knife!
BOY: Hit him, Dad!

(The LITTLE GIRL cries.)

LITTLE GIRL: Let's go home . . . let's go home. Don't fight.
MOTHER: It's his fault! If he hadn't come up to us!

BOY: Hit him, Dad!

(FATHER continues to beat OMBASI, who, in turn, responds to his blows. THEY roll in the sand. MOטHER tries to help her husband. SHE gets out of the car, picks up the bar, tries to strike hard, but ends up hitting her husband on the back. FATHER shrieks in pain. The BOY also gets out of the car and starts throwing sand at OMBASI with mediocre results, as some of it falls in FATHER's eyes. It is a quite an uproar. The LITTLE GIRL ends up getting out of the car as well, and watches the fight in fascination while eating her sandwich. Beside her, the BODY appears, a crab dangling from the corner of his mouth. He shakes his head at the spectacle. The LITTLE GIRL turns her gaze to the BODY. SHE offers him her sandwich. HE gently rejects her offer, removes the crab from his lips, and offers it to her. SHE takes the tiny animal, observing it curiously. Then, she drops it. The LITTLE GIRL and the BODY look at each other.)

LITTLE GIRL: Did he kill you?
BODY: No. I was killed along with many others, but I made it easy because I didn't take off my shoes.
LITTLE GIRL: Is he going to kill my Daddy?
BODY: No. Your father will lose an eye and you won't see him again.
LITTLE GIRL: You say silly things.
BODY: In my village, there were little girls like you, but their eyes were much older.
LITTLE GIRL: You say weird things.

(Faint at first, then louder and louder, grows the sound of an approaching helicopter. The BOY and MOTHER wave their arms.)

MOTHER: It's the Police! Helllllp! Hellllllllp!
BOY: This black man wants to kill us all!

(The sound grows louder and louder and the wind produced by the propeller creates whirlwinds of sand that surround and blind everyone. MOTHER and the BOY look up, but the two men, one white and one black, continue fighting while the sound of the rotor increases.)

14. A BEACH ALONG A SHORE OF NOTHINGNESS

The BODY sits in the sand, looking at the ocean. OMBASI comes on stage, naked.
HE sits beside THE BODY.

BODY: I told you.

OMBASI: Just be quiet. It wasn't like you said.

BODY: I was right.

OMBASI: No.

BODY: I told you that you'd drown in my shoes, didn't I?

OMBASI: But it wasn't like you said. I didn't drown in the sea.

BODY: Of course not, because in Madrid, there is no sea. But you drowned, even
if it was in a puddle.

OMBASI: I don't remember how it happened.

BODY: The cold. It's very cold in those gray cities. I told you that, too.

OMBASI: I was coughing, and my head hurt. I was hot. It was cold but I was hot.
I got dizzy. I fell down.

BODY: In a puddle. You'd fallen down in a puddle and drowned. Just like I told
you. People walked by and watched. And you drowned.

OMBASI: It's not like you said it would be.

BODY: Let's see, brother. I told you that you'd drown in my shoes, right? Well,
you drowned in my shoes. You shouldn't have taken them off me.

OMBASI: You didn't need them.

BODY: Neither do you, now.

OMBASI: They buried me in them.

BODY: What a waste.

OMBASI: Humph, they have more than enough shoes. They throw them away.

BODY: You shouldn't have gone back. They'd already rejected you. You shouldn't
have gone back.

OMBASI: What difference does it make now?

BODY: Right, what difference does it make? Since you were deported, you
should've stayed. Not everyone gets a second chance.

OMBASI: What happened to the man that I fought?

BODY: He lost an eye. He can't see out of his right eye. You were lucky they
deported you beforehand. If not, you would've gone to jail.

OMBASI: Why did he lose an eye?

BODY: He says it was your fault. You scratched him and sand got in it or
something. He started to cry and couldn't see. Now, he sees with the other
one.

OMBASI: It was his fault. Why did he hit me?

BODY: Hate.

OMBASI: I don't know why he had to hate me.

BODY: He hated himself.

OMBASI: He was an idiot.

BODY: That's why his wife left him.

OMBASI: Where did she go?

BODY: To the gray city where you drowned, with the kids. The man was left alone with only one eye.

OMBASI: Good. He seemed stupid. He was stupid.

BODY: And you, too, for going back. Come on, let's go.

OMBASI: Where?

BODY: Where else? Come on, your sister's there.

OMBASI: My sister? Why?

BODY: My brother killed her. She yelled at him and he hit her with a stick. You should've stayed.

OMBASI: What about your brother?

BODY: He's still there. He has a truck. Come on, let's go.

OMBASI: Alright, let's go. I want to see my sister.

BODY: She's very pretty. Pregnancy suits her well.

OMBASI: Was she pregnant?

BODY: She still is. Now she always will be.

OMBASI: Is she happy?

BODY: Yes. She'll be happy to see you. Come on, let's go.

(A door in the sea opens and through it come drums and sounds of an African celebration. The two naked men, cadavers now, go through it. The sound of the drums grows louder and the lights begin to fade.)

THE END

Ignacio del Moral's

A MOMMY AND A DADDY
(PAPIS)

Translated from the Spanish

by

Jartu Gallashaw Toles

CHARACTERS

MOM
DAD

A little square adorned with sparse vegetation and surrounded by asphalt is permeated with noise, smoke, and hustle. There is a bench, an overturned trash can, desolation and dog crap. Yet, despite it all, the birds continue their song. They are undisturbed by the disarray, or perhaps they are intoxicated by the things they are pecking.

Seated on the bench is DAD, who coos at a baby we do not see since she is inside a baby carriage. Then, he unfolds a newspaper and begins to read it, but pays little attention. He is continuously distracted by the child's gestures, which are indiscernible to the rest of the world.

Dodging obstacles after chancing her life at the tempestuous avenue intersection, MOM arrives at the haven with a similar carriage. DAD sees her and pretends not to notice her presence. Only when SHE is very close does HE raise his head and make a wan gesture of recognition.

MOM *(Smiling, approaches the bench)*: Hi. Let me see? *(Peeking into DAD's carriage)* Ooooh, how cute. She's grown since the last time. How long has it been?

DAD *(Quickly)*: Thirteen days . . . more or less.

MOM: Look how big she's gotten. Is it your turn again?

DAD: Well, yes . . . *(Smiling.)* Once again, attack of the feminist terror.

MOM: Oh, come on. I'm sure you love it.

(DAD makes a slight expression of doubt.)

DAD: And your baby?

MOM: Well, he still has a little cold. I'm not sure if it's an allergy.

DAD: Well, that's a shame. *(Peering into the carriage.)* He doesn't look bad.

MOM: He's better. But he's had some horrible days, poor little thing. You wouldn't believe the nights he's put us through. I caught a cold, too, walking around in that cold house.

DAD: Of course, that's why you haven't come out in so long.

MOM: It hasn't been that long. I came Friday and didn't see you.

DAD: Friday? Oh, Friday I had a meeting and I was running late.

MOM: I think I saw your wife. Well, at least I assumed she was your wife because she was with the baby.

DAD: Yes, maybe she decided to come here. Since it was nice out.

MOM: Yes, the weather was really nice. I thought you'd be here. I brought the photos I told you about, the ones of the seagulls.

DAD: Seagulls?

MOM: Yes, the ones I was thinking of including in my thesis.

DAD: Oh, right, the one you were doing on . . . on what? Something about lost seagulls.

MOM: On the changes in seagull migratory patterns.

DAD: The truth is that when it comes to birds, I can't tell a seagull from a duck.

MOM: I hardly remember myself. I haven't looked at my thesis in ages.

DAD: You should finish it. It's a very interesting subject.

MOM: You think so?

DAD: Sure. For example, I was always surprised to see seagulls at such a measly river as the Manzanares, so far from the sea. As soon as you finish it, I want to read it.

MOM: Impossible. With this little one and . . . well, it's impossible.

DAD: Oh. *(Cautiously)* You have a lot going on.

MOM *(Wanting to talk)*: Ooh, yes. If I were to tell you . . .

DAD *(Shyly)*: Sure. The lives we lead are so . . . well, to tell you the truth, sometimes I think our lives aren't going anywhere.

MOM: Right, it's true. *(Suddenly.)* Does your wife work?

DAD: Yes. But she has a very convenient schedule. Half of the time, she works at home. She does things for one of those consumer rights magazines. I think that's why she's so . . . demanding. Especially when it comes to her rights.

MOM: She's very pretty.

DAD *(Uncomfortable)*: Yes . . . and very intelligent, too.

MOM: Yes, it shows. You're lucky.

DAD *(With little enthusiasm)*: Yeah.

MOM: And she's lucky, too.

DAD: Thanks. I don't know if she'd agree.

MOM: How could she not agree? It's obvious that you help her out a lot.

DAD: The usual amount.

MOM: The usual amount is not at all, so . . .

DAD: Your husband is one of those who . . . ?

MOM: One of those who isn't around.

DAD: Are you separated?

MOM: No, but it's the same thing. He's never around. He's always traveling, doing lunches and dinners, going hunting . . .

DAD: I see. So, you spend a lot of time alone.

(She takes out a handkerchief and blows her nose. The sound seems to startle DAD's baby girl, whom he rocks gently.)

MOM: I'm sorry, I scared her. I have a cold. *(Pause.)* This little one has spent every night crying and I've had to get up, naked, of course. Imagine.

DAD: I can imagine. Um, I mean, what I mean is . . .

MOM (*Smiling*): You, too?

DAD: No. I usually sleep in a T-shirt.

MOM: No. What I meant was if you also get up at night, or does your wife do it.

DAD: Oh . . . well, it depends. Sometimes I do, sometimes she does. It just depends.

MOM: Of course. That makes sense. Especially if you two get along.

DAD (*Quickly*): Actually, I get up much more than she does. She doesn't hear the baby because there's construction going on next door and she sleeps with earplugs. Well, that's what she says. So, I have to get up more. Most nights I'm up doing a jig.

MOM: Well, it's a good thing you wear a T-shirt.

DAD: But on the other hand, I have to worry about my glasses. The baby cries. I wake up. I don't know how long she's been crying. I'm anxious. I feel for my glasses on the nightstand, crash, they fall on the floor; the baby is still crying. It seems like she's going to wake the neighbors. I try to find my glasses. I bend over and hit my forehead on the corner of the nightstand. I run off without my glasses to the baby's room; she's still crying. My right pinky toe hits the doorjamb. So, limping, and blind as a bat, I get to the baby's crib. She's lost her pacifier. I feel for the pacifier. It's on the floor, I don't know why. It has lint on it from the rug. What do I do?

MOM: Suck it clean and it's good as new.

DAD: Right. Clearly you're experienced at this.

MOM: For him, I put three or four pacifiers in the crib just in case, that way he always has one on hand. He's learned how to feel for it.

DAD: Hey, that's smart. That's a good idea. Of course, if I do the same with this one, her mother will think I'm spoiling her.

MOM: I warn you that it doesn't do me any good. He cries just the same, because his problem isn't the pacifier, but that his nose is stopped up, or he gets colicky, like they do.

DAD: Or has gas.

MOM: Or gas. You've also had to deal with the infamous gas?

DAD: Well . . . For a time I had a lot, when I stopped smoking . . . The doctor said I was nervous, but . . . (*Seeing her expression.*) You were referring to the baby, I'm afraid.

MOM (*Smiling*): We always talk about them, don't we?

DAD: Sure. They turn into our obsession. We don't know how to talk about anything else.

MOM: Right, it seems there is no other subject. Especially for us. We drop everything for them.

DAD: For example, the lost seagulls.

MOM: For example.

DAD: But the seagulls stay there, flying around above the dumpsters along the M-30 bypass.

MOM: Everything keeps on going, even if we forget.

DAD: Maybe they're an alibi.

MOM: For what?

DAD: I don't know. So we don't have to face . . . *(HE shrugs his shoulders.)* certain things.

(ONE of the children cries. BOTH PARENTS rush to tend to their respective child.)

MOM: He's teething.

DAD *(Picking up his child.)*: And she's showing her sympathy. *(Looks at his watch.)* It's about time for her to eat.

(THEY both rock their children and talk over the crying. Looking at each other over their babies' little heads, THEY laugh.)

MOM: Sometimes I understand the people who throw them out the window.

DAD: Me, too. I don't know how we put up with them.

MOM: Maybe they're our salvation. Maybe without them we'd be lost, right? And we'd have to put up with ourselves.

DAD: Well, I have to get back. This one is starving and her mother will fuss if she doesn't eat when she's supposed to. *(Putting the baby girl in the carriage.)*

MOM: Yes, I'll be going pretty soon as well.

(DAD gets ready to leave.)

DAD: Alright, well, see you. If you come tomorrow.

MOM: Yes, I'll come. Well, if nothing happens.

DAD: Well, remember to bring the pictures. I'm really interested in seeing them.

MOM: Really? Every time I try to show them to someone, they look at me like I'm crazy.

DAD: Don't pay any attention. There they are, poor things, along the M-30 bypass, eating trash and waiting for someone to remember them.

(DAD looks at his watch, makes a gesture of alarm, and waving goodbye, starts to leave. MOM watches him leave.)

MOM *(Calling him.)*: Hey!

(DAD turns around. MOM starts to tell him something, but the frenzied siren of a passing ambulance stops her.)

DAD: Huh?
MOM: Nothing! See you tomorrow!

(DAD moves farther away. MOM watches him leave. SHE takes the baby boy from his carriage and holds him in her arms. SHE looks up into the sky. The sound of seagulls is heard, and SHE sobs softly.)

THE END

Ignacio del Moral's

LITTLE BEARS
(OSEZNOS)

Translated from the Spanish

by

Jartu Gallashaw Toles

CHARACTERS

ENRIQUE
MIGUEL
ANGEL

Evening.

Enter three boys, revealing their enviable age with the chuckling and clumsiness characteristic of somewhat tipsy, beer bottle-toting adolescents. Their enormous feet are clad in flip-flops, and they exhibit a free flow of foul language, laughter, and a desperate zeal for fun. One of them carries a huge stuffed bear, holding the four-legged creature as if it could reciprocate with its proverbially fatal embrace or, as if it could keep the boy from his imminent fall, considering the poor guy has a drop more of alcohol in his system than he needs or can handle.

For that reason he is quite a nuisance. His friends—although not in very good condition themselves—follow him, combining their youthful and drunken solidarity with a cruelty that incites laughter at the expense of someone else.

Finally, the unfortunate ENRIQUE—such is the name of the drunken adolescent—falls to the ground. He tumbles, holding tight to the bear, which causes enormous amusement in MIGUEL and ANGEL, the two other idlers.

MIGUEL: Jeez, you sure do like that bear of yours! It's like you want to screw it or something!

ENRIQUE: Well, yeah! So what if I do? I found it and it's mine, right? And with it I can do whatever I feel like. If I want to screw it, I will. You got a problem with that?

ANGEL: If I got a problem with it, he says. Whoa, sure seems like you feel like it. Come on, stand up and let's see if we can still catch up with the chicks.

ENRIQUE: No.

ANGEL: What do you mean? You're planning on staying here or what?

ENRIQUE: Yes.

MIGUEL: This guy is an asshole.

ANGEL: Come on, don't be a blockhead. You'll see, when you talk to her.

ENRIQUE: I said no, I'm staying.

MIGUEL: There's no convincing him. Grab him on that side and I'll grab him over here and we'll carry him. It's getting late and my old man's at home today.

(MIGUEL AND ANGEL try to grab ENRIQUE, who wriggles furiously.)

ENRIQUE: I said no! Leave me alone, you fags!

ANGEL: Come on, Ricky, damn. Don't be an asshole!

ENRIQUE: Your father's an asshole! Leave me alone. I want to stay here.

ANGEL: Damn, it's not that serious. You'll see, tomorrow he'll be as good as new.

ENRIQUE: Go to hell! She and that cousin of hers who screwed everything up.

ANGEL: Alright, but let's go.

ENRIQUE: No!

(MIGUEL is bent over trying to grab onto ENRIQUE by the legs. In one swift movement from his position on the ground ENRIQUE kicks MIGUEL in the mouth.)

MIGUEL: Aaah! *(Bringing his hand to his mouth.)* I'm bleeding, you son of a bitch! *(Then HE kicks ENRIQUE.)*
ANGEL: What are you doing? Can't you see he didn't do it on purpose?
ENRIQUE: He didn't hurt me. He kicked the bear.
MIGUEL: Because of this asshole the girls are going to leave!
ENRIQUE *(Struggling to get on his feet)*: You know what I say about girls?

(Before MIGUEL can get one word out, ENRIQUE heaves on him a spew of vomit, consisting of beer, hamburger, and some other element of dubious gastronomic origin.)

MIGUEL: Aaah! Asshole, son of a bitch! God, that's sick! This guy's a pig! I'm gonna kill you! *(HE punches ENRIQUE, who responds furiously. THEY both give free reign to accumulated rage and animosity.)*
ANGEL *(Trying to separate them)*: Chill out, dammit! That's enough! We're pals, right? That's enough, dammit!

(At last ENRIQUE falls to the ground. When MIGUEL charges at him, ANGEL stops him.)

MIGUEL: Get out of my way, this guy's asking for it!
ANGEL: Chill out, already, damn! *(Smelling him.)* God, look at you.
(And unable to help it, ANGEL bursts into laughter. ENRIQUE laughs from the ground as well. MIGUEL, puked on, and very fed up, looks at them.)
MIGUEL: Go to hell! *(Furious, HE makes a motion to leave.)*
ANGEL: Where are you going? Man, wait!
MIGUEL: Just forget about me!
ANGEL: But, dude . . . !

(ANGEL tries to stop MIGUEL. MIGUEL turns around and shoves him.)

MIGUEL: I said leave me alone! Look what this asshole did to me! Dammit, they're gonna be on my back at home.
ENRIQUE: Let him go! He stinks!

(MIGUEL, furious, throws himself on ENRIQUE, intending to hit him. ANGEL grabs on to him.)

ANGEL *(To ENRIQUE)*: You, shut up! *(To MIGUEL.)* He didn't get too much on you. You can wash off in a fountain and then . . .

MIGUEL: And then I'm going to see if I can still catch the girls, who've left because of this idiot. All along I was trying to hook up and this asshole had to come along and screw everything up, just when we were about to hook up with them!

ENRIQUE *(Absurdly conciliatory)*: I'm sorry, man, really. Look, I'll let you have the bear. Forget about women, really. I bet I'm right . . . right, Angel?

(MIGUEL, furious, grabs the bear and hits ENRIQUE with it.)

MIGUEL: Go to hell! Go straight to hell!

ENRIQUE: Jesus, man, it's for your own good! Angel! Tell him it's for his own good!

ANGEL: Goddammit! Enough already, Ricky. You, stop it, you're going to hurt him.

MIGUEL: I'm going home. This faggot's already screwed up my whole afternoon. Are you coming with me or are you staying?

ANGEL: I can't go back without him. We're neighbors.

MIGUEL: Well, you can both go screw yourselves. It'll take an hour to get there and if I'm late checking in, I'm in deep shit, you know how paranoid they are at home about the gypsies in our building.

ANGEL: Wait a minute, Jesus! It's still early!

MIGUEL: I don't feel like it, dammit! *(MIGUEL leaves.)*

ENRIQUE: Miguel, hey Miguel! Don't leave, don't screw around! *(To ANGEL.)* He left, the little twit.

ANGEL *(Seeing MIGUEL leave)*: Miguel! Wait, dammit! (*When HE realizes that MIGUEL isn't coming back, HE turns around, discouraged. Seeing ENRIQUE cuddled up on the ground with the bear, HE kicks a piece of rubble, disheartened.)* Shit!

ENRIQUE: Shhhh! Don't start screaming now like a crazy person. I'm going to sleep.

ANGEL: Put a sock in it and let's go home. After all, we've wasted the afternoon.

ENRIQUE: I haven't wasted anything. Let me sleep. I don't want to go home. Screw them. You know what? I'm sure they wouldn't give a damn if I didn't go back.

ANGEL: Let's not start again.

ENRIQUE: I'm fucking great. You got it? Fucking great.

ANGEL: Come on, get up. I'll take you.

ENRIQUE: No.

ANGEL: No, if we miss the bus, you'll see. *(Trying to lift ENRIQUE off the ground, not an easy task due to the excessive mass and fur of the damn bear.)* Look, man, either you come with me or I'm going to beat you so bad they'll have to take you in the ambulance. Put the bear down, dammit!

ENRIQUE: I don't want to, hell! I found it right. Well, it's mine. I saved it from the dumpster, didn't I?

(ANGEL, exasperated, lets him fall. ENRIQUE hits the ground and moans. ANGEL hesitates at the sight of him.)

ENRIQUE: Why do people throw so many things in the dumpsters? Last year my folks fixed up the bathroom and had to call for a dumpster, for the debris. Well, the next morning it was full of stuff. Even a sofa and a mattress full of pis stains. Or cum! *(He laughs.)*

ANGEL: That's nothing. On my street they found a little kid, don't you remember? If he'd been there any longer they would've thrown him in the trash truck.

ENRIQUE: Just like the bear. If I hadn't come to get it, it would've gone into the truck.

ANGEL: Stop kidding around. That doesn't even compare.

ENRIQUE: Shhhhh! Man, you're not gonna believe it, but I can feel the Earth's rotation. Everything's spinning. I swear.

ANGEL: That's because you're wasted. Look at the sky and you'll see.

ENRIQUE *(Rolling over, face up)*: It's spinning, too. It's almost dark, but only two or three stars will come out.

ANGEL *(Sprawling out beside him)*: You can't see them because of the pollution.

ENRIQUE: Where my mom is from, there are loads of stars.

ANGEL: Yeah, in small towns there are lots of stars. And at the ocean, too.

ENRIQUE: But aside from that, small towns are shitty. And you get dizzy at the ocean.

ANGEL: You get dizzy here, too, don't you? You are dizzy.

ENRIQUE: Well, alright, but that's because I'm wasted. It's not the same. If you fall here you don't drown. You might step on dog shit, but you won't drown.

ANGEL: Well, I plan on going some place where there's an ocean. I'm not staying here.

ENRIQUE: That's what you say now. *(Looking toward the sky.)* They're hardly any. Only the Big Dipper . . . the Ursa Major . . . Hey, bear! Look, your mother. She's in heaven. She probably died.

ANGEL: Alright, that's enough.

ENRIQUE: Ah, that's right. Sorry. You're both orphans. You're one because of your mother and he's one because of his mom. Look, bear, another orphan. But in small towns you die from the lack of action.

ANGEL: Really, man, I've known you my whole life and it still surprises me what an asshole you are.

ENRIQUE: Yeah, I surprise myself, too.

ANGEL: I have to wake up early tomorrow. I have class. Besides, we're going to get home late, and when the neighbors see you like this, they're gonna think you're a junkie and we'll get our asses kicked.

ENRIQUE: Go if you want to. I can't get up.

ANGEL: If you let go of the bear . . .

ENRIQUE: I can't, it's for my mother. You don't understand that, but you give mothers gifts to keep them happy.

ANGEL: But it's a piece of shit! How is she going to be happy about this piece of crap?

ENRIQUE: It doesn't matter. It can be washed. She'd wash it anyway, even if it were bought. She'd say that anybody could've had it and it has germs. She's very meticulous . . . washes everything. She buys clothes and washes them before we wear them. She washes my sister's toys, too, as soon as she brings them from the park. Half of them get messed up, but the half that's left is clean. So as soon as the bear gets home, it goes straight into the washer. Its eyes will fall off, but that doesn't matter. The important thing is that it goes in the washer.

ANGEL: It won't fit.

ENRIQUE: Uh huh, if you fold it like this, see?

ANGEL: It won't fit.

ENRIQUE: It will. The washer in my house is really big. It'll even wash the rugs.

ANGEL: But this bear is really big. It's huge.

ENRIQUE: Damn, then, she'll cut it in half and sew it back up. I'm telling you she'll wash it. Or she'll wash it in the bathtub. Alright?

ANGEL: Fine. It's gonna get messed up. If it gets messed up, it will be useless.

ENRIQUE: So, what do you care? Is it your mother? Is it your bathtub? Is it your bear? Well, then! What do you care?

ANGEL: Me? Not a hoot.

ENRIQUE: Well, then. Leave me alone. It seems like it bothers you that I'm taking a bear to my mother.

ANGEL: I don't know why it would bother me.

ENRIQUE: I don't know. Because you don't have a mother, maybe. Hey, Angel, I have to tell you something.

ANGEL *(Resignedly)*: What.

ENRIQUE: I'm really sorry you don't have a mother.

ANGEL: I'm used to it.

ENRIQUE: No, dammit, seriously, it must be weird not to have a mother. See? When you have one, you don't care, because they're a pain in the neck, but when you don't have one . . .

ANGEL: Okay, fine, drop it.

ENRIQUE: Anyway, don't worry. There are lots of people who have mothers and are worse off.

ANGEL: I'm not worried about it, alright. Jesus.

ENRIQUE: It's just that . . . damn, I feel bad that you don't have a mother.

ANGEL: Alright, fine. I feel bad you don't have a brain, and that I'm not going to beat the crap out of you.

ENRIQUE: Well, everybody needs something.

ANGEL: Something? Lots of things.

ENRIQUE: That's true. And today's Daily Double for $1000: "Things We Need". Girls.

ANGEL: Stars.

ENRIQUE: Girls.

ANGEL: An ocean to drown in.

ENRIQUE: And girls. Don't forget about girls.

ANGEL: Space.

ENRIQUE: Girls.

ANGEL: A future.

ENRIQUE: Screw it.

ANGEL: Well, yeah, we do also need to screw.

ENRIQUE: No, I mean screw like when you say screw, not *screw* screw. But yeah, we could use a good screw. Hey, where will we be in ten years?

ANGEL: What do I know? Maybe we'll be dead.

ENRIQUE: Don't screw around, man. I'll be in a villa doing Marta Sanchez. Well, no, by then she'll be an old lady.

ANGEL: Yeah if you haven't died of some kind of cancer.

ENRIQUE: Jesus, why would I die of cancer?

ANGEL: Well, you could crack your skull on a motorcycle.

ENRIQUE: But man, what does that have to do with anything?

ANGEL: Nothing. You said where would we be in ten years: Daily Double for $1000: "Place You Will Be In Ten Years". A junkie on the streets.

ENRIQUE: Don't mess around: In a car with a phone.

ANGEL: In jail with AIDS.

ENRIQUE: On a yacht in Mallorca with two topless babes.

ANGEL: Working in a burger joint.

ENRIQUE: Hell, no. On an island that I bought because I won the lottery.

ANGEL: Married to a girl who got pregnant the first time you did her.

ENRIQUE: Doing 100 on a bike with a 1500 engine that I saw the other day that was so cool.

ANGEL: You know what? You're a mess. I don't know why I'm still your friend.

ENRIQUE: You know something else? You're such a drip. Must be because you don't have a mother. I don't know why I keep being your friend either.

ANGEL: Must be because I'm a tough dude.

ENRIQUE: Must be. I'm also a tough dude.

ANGEL: Well, fine.

ENRIQUE: No, seriously. I know it seems faggoty, but the truth is, I love you.

ANGEL: Oh, screw that . . .

ENRIQUE: Screwing, no. I love you but that's it. And don't you think that having a mother is all that. All they do is drive you up the wall. I think mothers are essential until you get older. Then, what you need are friends.

ANGEL: Shut up, will you?

ENRIQUE: It's just that I really love you. You care about me.

ANGEL: You know, I'm going to smack you good for being a faggot.

ENRIQUE: No, man, don't get confused. It's just that it gets harder and harder to tell someone something like that. Only to girls, and when you say it, it either sounds like a lie or is a lie. But you have to say it so they'll let you do stuff. On the other hand, with your close friends, you can. Come on, I say you can. At least, when you're wasted.

ANGEL: Alright, fine. Come on, let's go.

ENRIQUE *(Stands up)*: Yeah, let's go. I'm better now. I'm better. Jesus! I don't know what I'll be doing in ten years, but now I'm fucking great. Fucking great! *(And with energy emanating from all pores, ENRIQUE begins kicking the trash cans.)*

ANGEL *(Laughing)*: What are you doing? Are you nuts?

ENRIQUE: No, man! I'm just happy! Throw me the bear!

(ENRIQUE throws it to ANGEL so that he'll throw it back. ANGEL throws it and ENRIQUE finishes it off with one kick. The bear soars. They both laugh.)

ANGEL *(In the voice of John Madden)*: "The bear scores a touchdownnn! Yeah baby, goooooooo!"

ENRIQUE: "With a swift kick in the asssss!"

(ENRIQUE goes to pick up the bear. ANGEL jumps on top of him and they volley the four-legged creature, laughing and hitting it, until it tears, allowing its contents to fall out, covering them both. Laughing and punching each other playfully, they exit the stage, leaving behind a trail of vomit, broken

glass, scattered trash, sawdust and a crude tenderness of a nightfall that, if you look hard enough, could really be beautiful.)

THE END

ABOUT THE TRANSLATOR

Jartu Gallashaw Toles, a native of Fort Valley, Georgia, graduated with honors from Clark Atlanta University with a Bachelor of Arts in Spanish in 1997. She received a Master of Arts in Spanish/Option in Translation from Rutgers, The State University of New Jersey in 1999 and in the same year was awarded the American Translators Association Student Award for her translation of *Dark Man's Gaze*. Toles has been in the interpreting industry since 1996 and is the founder and owner of Modern Linguistic Solutions, Inc., which provides translation, interpreting, and transcription services in Atlanta, Georgia.

TRANSLATOR'S ACKNOWLEDGEMENTS

Sincerest thanks and appreciation to everyone who supported me in the effort to make these translations possible, specifically Dr. Phyllis Zatlin. Thank you for your guidance and insight during my graduate career, and thank you for this great opportunity. Also, I give greatest appreciation to Ignacio del Moral for permission to translate his delightful plays and his assistance during the thesis process. Special thanks to Ana Angulo for her insight on Castilian slang, and to Gabrielle Talley for her helpful encouragement. Eric Ruffin, thank you for your enormous contribution. Likewise, I would like to thank both the editor and Christine Jenack for their time and effort in the preparation of this edition and the Program for Cultural Cooperation Between Spain's Ministry of Education, Culture and Sports and United States Universities for their support of this project.

J. G. T.

CRITICAL REACTION TO THE PLAY

"Ignacio del Moral characterizes *La mirada del hombre oscuro* (*Dark Man's Gaze*) as `a fable about lack of communication,' a lack caused by fear and hatred that leads to racism. The work parodies the reaction of a middle-class family upon encountering the Other, in this case, African emigrants who have come to Spain seeking work."

Camilla Stevens
Entre actos: Diálogos sobre teatro español entre siglos
(University Park, PA), 1999

Dark Man's Gaze is "a work of great thematic and formal interest that ably combines an agile dramatic structure, vivid dialogue, and a rapid-fire action with an oneiric element that plays with time and image. Its theme is anti-racist, lively and timely." It is an entertaining comedy "with touches of tenderness and a backdrop of social tragedy. This work rises above general groups and `alternate' genres to achieve a universality that makes it a part of our theatre's contemporary history."

María-José Ragué-Arias
El teatro de fin de milenio en España
(Barcelona), 1996

Director Ernesto Caballero "converts the stage into two well-defined visual worlds: the lower, closed and empty one occupied by the immigrant; the upper, open and promising one occupied by the family. The intrusion of one character or another into the other's territory is made in an intentionally strained, even physically difficult manner. Nevertheless, the director succeeds in giving geographic and aesthetic unity to these spaces."

Miguel Medina Vicario
Reseña (Madrid)
March 1993

Dark Man's Gaze is "a stimulating show, entertaining in its acerbic criticism, while at the same time proof, once again, that we have first rate authors, directors and actors capable of creating unforgettable performances like this one."

Enrique Centeno
Diario 16 (Madrid)
January 1993

In *A Mommy and a Daddy*, "Ignacio del Moral has constructed a lively, somewhat melancholy dialogue through which two people, a man and a woman, find each other and express their longings while they take their respective babies for a stroll. Loneliness and touches of sadness resonate with gentle humor."

Three neighborhood boys appear in Del Moral's *Little Bears*. "One of the gang is drunk. That circumstance allows the author, who uses this social group's lexicon, to air the first sufferings that young people experience after their first passions."

Juanjo Guerrenabarrena
El Público (Madrid)
May/June 1992

ESTRENO: CONTEMPORARY SPANISH PLAYS SERIES

No. 10   Alfonso Sastre: **The Abandoned Doll. Young Billy Tell.** (*Historia de una muñeca abandonada. El único hijo de William Tell*).
Translated by Carys Evans-Corrales. 1996.
ISBN: 1-888463-00-7

No. 11   Lauro Olmo and Pilar Encisco: **The Lion Calls a Meeting. The Lion Foiled. The Lion in Love.** (*Asamblea general. Los leones*)
Translated by Carys Evans-Corrales. 1997.
ISBN: 1-888463-01-5

No. 12   José Luis Alonso de Santos: **Hostages in the Barrio.** (*La estanquera de Vallecas*).
Translated by Phyllis Zatlin. 1997.
ISBN: 1-888463-02-3

No. 13   Fermín Cabal: **Passage.** (*Travesía*)
Translated by H. Rick Hite. 1998.
ISBN: 1-888463-03-1

No. 14   Antonio Buero-Vallejo: **The Sleep of Reason** (*El sueño de la razón*)
Translated by Marion Peter Holt. 1998.
ISBN: 1-888463-04-X

No. 15   Fernando Arrabal: **The Body-Builder's Book of Love** (*Breviario de amor de un halterófilo*)
Translated by Lorenzo Mans. 1999.
ISBN: 1-888463-05-8

No. 16   Luis Araújo: **Vanzetti**
Translated by Mary-Alice Lessing. 1999.
ISBN: 1-888463-08-2

No. 17   Josep M. Benet i Jornet: **Legacy** (*Testament*)
Translated by Janet DeCesaris. 2000.
ISBN: 1-888463-09-0

No. 18   Sebastián Junyent: **Packing up the Past** (*Hay que deshacer la casa*)
Translated by Ana Mengual. 2000.
ISBN: 1-888463-10-4

ORDER INFORMATION

List price, nos. 1-11: $6; nos. 12-27 & rev. 6, $8.
Shipping and handling for one or two volumes, $1.25 each.
Free postage on orders of three or more volumes, within United States.
Special price for complete set of 27 volumes, $125.

Make checks payable to ESTRENO Plays and send to:

ESTRENO Plays, Dept. of Spanish & Portuguese
Rutgers, The State University of New Jersey
105 George St.
New Brunswick, NJ 08901-1414, USA

For information on discounts available to distributors and to college bookstores for
textbook orders, and for estimates on postage outside the United States, contact:

E-mail: estrplay@rci.rutgers.edu
Phone: 1-732-932-9412 extension 25
FAX: 1-732-932-9837

VISIT OUR WEBSITE:

www.rci.rutgers.edu/~estrplay/webpage.html

ESTRENO Plays is printed at Ag Press in Manhattan, Kansas.